KidCaps' Presents
A Kids Guide to American History
Volume 2
Trail of Tears to the Gold Rush

KidCaps is An Imprint of BookCaps™

www.bookcaps.com

© 2012. All Rights Reserved.

Table of Contents

ABOUT KIDCAPS 4

INTRODUCTION 5

TRAIL OF TEARS 6

    CHAPTER 1 7

    CHAPTER 2 15

    CHAPTER 3 16

        1831- Choctaw Tribe 16

        1832- Seminole Tribe 17

        1834- Creek Tribe 17

        1837- Chickasaw Tribe 18

        1838- Cherokee Tribe 19

    CHAPTER 4 21

        The White Child of a Settler 21

        The Child of a Native American 21

    CHAPTER 5 23

        Conclusion 25

THE PONY EXPRESS 27

    INTRODUCTION 28

    CHAPTER 1: WHAT LED UP TO THE PONY EXPRESS? 30

    CHAPTER 2: WHY DID THE PONY EXPRESS HAPPEN? 32

    CHAPTER 3: WHAT HAPPENED DURING THE DAYS OF THE PONY EXPRESS? 34

    CHAPTER 4: WHAT WAS IT LIKE TO BE A KID DURING THE PONY EXPRESS? 38

    CHAPTER 5: HOW DID THE PONY EXPRESS END? 40

    CHAPTER 6: WHAT HAPPENED AFTER THE PONY EXPRESS? 42

    CONCLUSION 44

THE UNDERGROUND RAILROAD 46

    INTRODUCTION 48

    CHAPTER 1: WHAT LED UP TO THE UNDERGROUND RAILROAD? 50

    CHAPTER 2: WHY DID THE UNDERGROUND RAILROAD HAPPEN? 56

    CHAPTER 3: WHAT HAPPENED ON THE UNDERGROUND RAILROAD? 58

    CHAPTER 4: WHAT WAS IT LIKE TO BE A KID DURING THE TIME OF THE UNDERGROUND RAILROAD? 62

    CHAPTER 5: HOW DID THE UNDERGROUND RAILROAD COME TO AN END? 62

    CHAPTER 6: WHAT HAPPENED AFTER THE UNDERGROUND RAILROAD? 65

    CONCLUSION 68

THE CALIFORNIA GOLD RUSH 69

    INTRODUCTION 71

    CHAPTER 1: WHAT LED UP TO THE GOLD RUSH? 74

    CHAPTER 2: WHY DID THE GOLD RUSH HAPPEN? 77

    CHAPTER 3: WHAT HAPPENED DURING THE GOLD RUSH? 80

    CHAPTER 4: WHAT WAS IT LIKE TO BE A KID DURING THE GOLD RUSH? 85

    CHAPTER 5: HOW DID THE GOLD RUSH END? 86

CHAPTER 6: WHAT HAPPENED AFTER THE GOLD RUSH?..88
CONCLUSION 91

About KidCaps

KidCaps is an imprint of BookCaps™ that is just for kids! Each month BookCaps will be releasing several books in this exciting imprint. Visit are website or like us on Facebook to see more!

Introduction

This book is a compilation of four previously published KidCaps books. It is the first in a two volume series. It is published as a bundled for discount pricing.

Trail of Tears

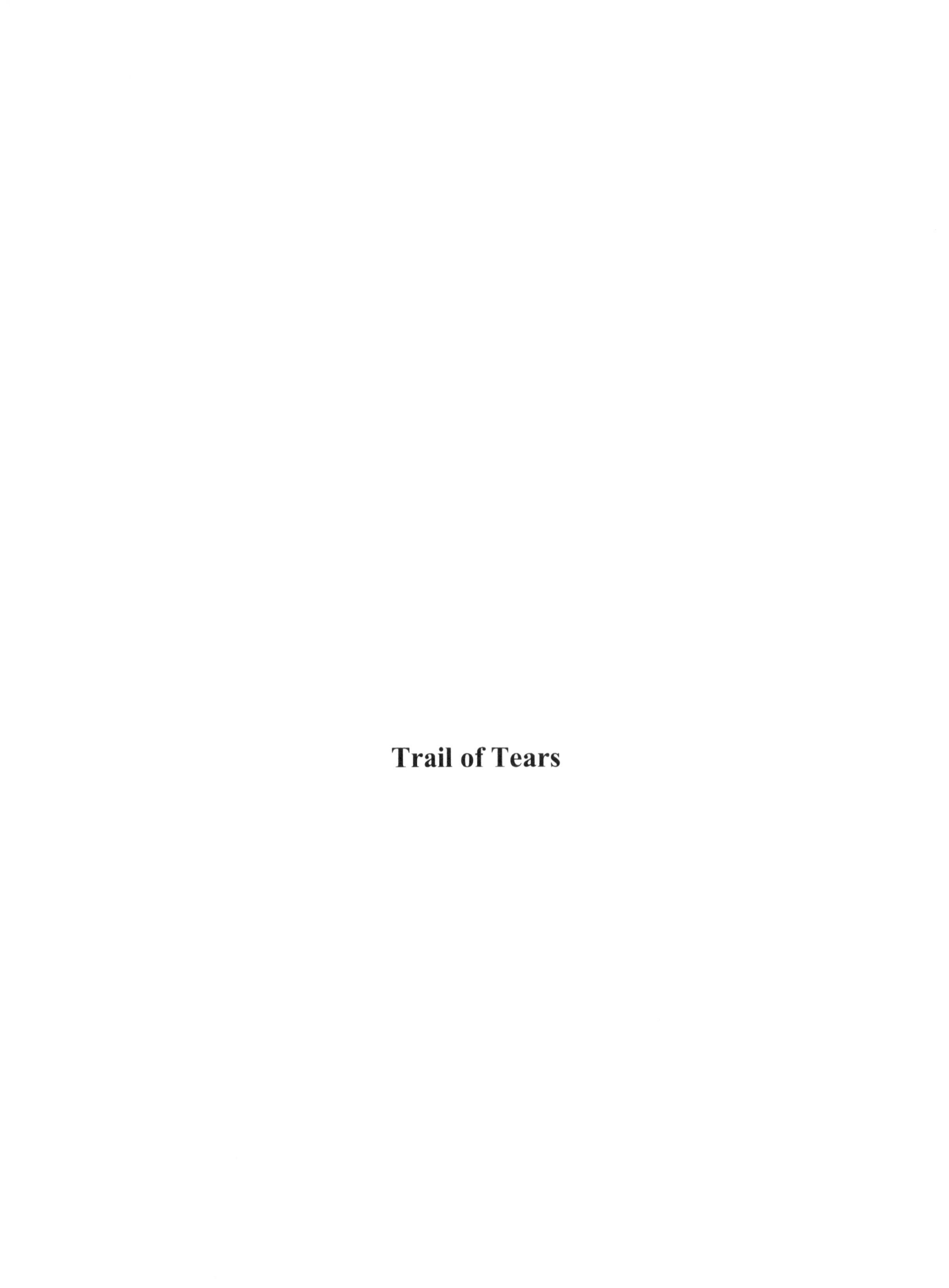

Chapter 1

"Nu na hi du na tlo hi lu I".

Do you know what those words mean? They are in a language originally spoken by a tribe of Native Americans called the Cherokee. In English, these words mean: "The Trail Where They Cried." Sounds pretty sad, right? Well, no doubt you have a few questions about this very famous trail. For example, you might wonder: what was this "trail" and who were the persons crying? What led up to these persons walking on this trail, and where did the trail lead to? What was it like to be a kid during those times?

Well, to answer these important questions, we are going to take a look back at part of the history of the United States of America, specifically the years 1831 to 1838, although we'll also look at some events a little before and a little after. We will especially be looking at the treatment of Native Americans, or, as they were once called, Indians.

Let's start with a little background information. Do you know who one of the first Europeans was to really explore what is now called the United States? Well, most of us know that Christopher Columbus was the first person to let Europe know about what he called "the New World." However, Columbus spent most of his time in the Caribbean Sea, on islands like Hispaniola and in the Bahamas. He never really got to spend a lot of time in what is now the United States.

However, about 30 years after Christopher Columbus died, an explorer from Europe named Hernando de Soto decided to see how big this new area of land really was. Starting out in Florida, de Soto wanted to explore more and to travel deeper and deeper into the new territory. He went north to the areas now called Georgia and South Carolina, and then he went as far west as the Mississippi river. In fact, he is thought to be the first European ever to cross this huge river! It took him and his men about a month to make the rafts and to actually cross it!

This explorer learned a lot about this new land, but there is a darker side to de Soto's tale. You see, when he arrived in Florida in May of 1539 and started to explore the area north and west, he brought with him 620 men, 220 horses, lots of weapons, and even engineers to build things. Why did he bring so many people with him? Well, Hernando de Soto wasn't only interested in exploring; he also wanted to *conquer* the new land, no matter who or what stood in his way. He had already found a lot of gold in South America, and he was convinced that, within four years or so, he would be able to conquer the entire American continent and make Spain even richer! But when de Soto arrived in Florida and started to explore, he quickly found that he wasn't the first person to walk on this continent.

In fact, he was actually the newest arrival.

For thousands of years, Native Americans had been living on the American continent. They had been raising crops, having children, fishing, hunting, and even fighting wars. They had their own religion, they loved, they hated, they lived, and they died. Native Americans stretched from the present day state of Washington all the way to Georgia; and from Maine to California. In fact, when de Soto landed with his men in Florida in 1539, there were approximately 10 million Native Americans living all across the continent.

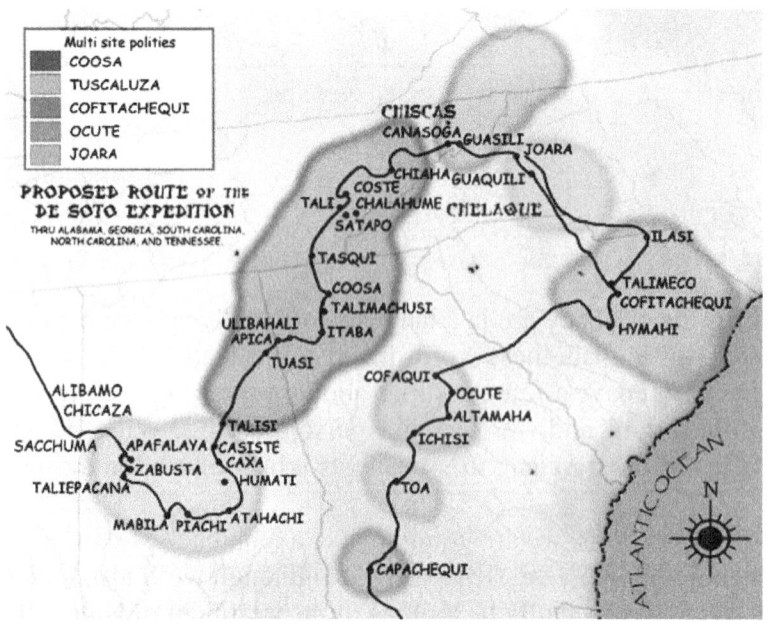

Hernando de Soto's route through the American Continent

How did Hernando de Soto and his men treat the people who were living on the land that they wanted? Well, let's take as an example what happened a few months after he arrived. After having moved north, then west, and then south again, de Soto came to a small fortress town called Mabila, in modern-day Alabama. He was looking for supplies, but the chief who had been helping him stopped talking to him and left to another room. Another Native American was brought in to help, but he ended up being mistreated by one of de Soto's soldiers. This soldier actually got to the point of hitting the Native American with his sword and breaking open the skin on his back. The rest of the people in the fortress town immediately fought to defend themselves against what they perceived to be an attack. The result? After nine bloody hthe ground.

Hernando de Soto's men attacking Mabila

~~We can see from this example~~ what has often been the result of people coming to the American continent. Like de Soto, many came with big plans: they wanted to find gold, to plant cotton, and to raise cattle- but the Native Americans who were already there were, in the newcomer's eyes, keeping the settlers from reaching their goals. In this report, we are going to learn about how good people, many of them white Americans, fell into that same old trap of mistreating Native Americans just so that they could get some more money or some more land. Sadly, Hernando de Soto was not the first person to abuse the Native Americans, nor would he be the last.

In the United States, this aggression really culminated in what we mentioned earlier: the Trail of Tears. What was the Trail of Tears? Well, this term, translated from a Cherokee phrase, refers to the forced relocation of Native American tribes, specifically those living in the Southeast United States, from 1831-1838.

Why was this forced relocation referred to as a "Trail of Tears"? Unfortunately, not everyone who started the journey finished it. What's more, most of the people who left their homes did so against their choice. They cried because of the death, and they cried because they were sad to leave their homes. That is why there were so many tears shed on this trail.

Let's learn more about the Trail of Tears. We are going to be talking about some of the things that culminated in the forced relocation of more than 15,000 Native Americans. Here are some keywords that will be very important: we will talk about the Louisiana Purchase, and how it changed the way that people looked at difficulties associated with sharing resources with Native Americans (or, as they called it back then, "the Indian problem"). We will also learn about an interesting philosophy that a lot of people, even presidents, had. This philosophy was called "Manifest Destiny". Finally, we will see how the U.S. Federal government finally got involved in 1830 and took action against the Native Americans by passing a law called the Indian Removal Act.

There is a lot of really interesting stuff to talk about, so let's get started!

What led up to the Trail of Tears?

Basically, the Native Americans that would eventually walk the trail of tears and that would be forced out of their homeland were the victims of three separate attacks against them. Each of the attacks by themselves was bad enough, but together, these three problems spelled the end of life as they knew it for many Native Americans. Here were the three problems:

- White settlers felt that they were entitled to take Native American lands because of a philosophy called "Manifest Destiny"
- Native Americans were not viewed as people the same way white settlers were.
- Andrew Jackson, the President of the United States from 1829-1837, was very biased against Native Americans because of his past experience fighting wars against them.

PROBLEM 1: WHITE SETTLERS FELT THAT THEY WERE ENTITLED TO TAKE NATIVE AMERICAN LANDS BECAUSE OF A PHILOSOPHY CALLED "MANIFEST DESTINY"

After the War of 1812 had ended, and the citizens of the United States began to enjoy the peace and prosperity that came with their resource-rich country, many people wanted to start pushing westward, to see what new treasures they could find. This desire only grew larger when the United States bought a large portion of land in 1803 in a transaction called the Louisiana Purchase. With so much new land to explore, settlers began to push west by the thousands. In fact, they began to think that they had some sort of a right to the land, something they called Manifest Destiny. What did that phrase mean?

Well, we usually use the word "destiny" when we are talking about love, right? When we think that two people make a great couple, we say that it was "destiny", or that they were *meant* to be together. That's kind of what people thought back in the 1800s. They felt that Americans had a special right to dominate the entire continent, all the way to the Pacific Ocean. What's more, they thought that if anyone got in the settler's way, that they were interfering with their destiny, and that was just a huge problem.

A picture showing the American thought about their Manifest Destiny to move westward

PROBLEM 2: NATIVE AMERICANS WERE NOT VIEWED THE SAME WAY AS WHITE SETTLERS WERE.

As we saw in the introduction, the Europeans who arrived on the American continent, and even those Americans who were born there later, never really learned to get along with the Native Americans. In fact, they still called them "Indians" (after Christopher Columbus' mistake of thinking he had landed in India). Most people viewed the Native Americans as just being in the way of their getting what they wanted.

Some settlers, however, took their dislike of Native Americans even further. Why was this?

Native Americans did not have the same background as Europeans. For example, they did not practice the same religion as most of the original colonists and of the people later born in the U.S. Most of these had been and were Christian; and that meant that they went to church on Sundays and celebrated holidays like Christmas and Easter. Native Americans, however, did not base their faith on a holy book, like the Bible. Rather, every moment of their lives was spent trying to live on harmony with what they perceived as a universal force around them. They believed that the Creator was omnipresent (was everywhere and in everything) and could be worshipped anywhere. For Christians who only worshipped on Sundays and only prayed in a church, this was a very strange way of religion. What's more, Native Americans dressed diff

A Seminole warrior

Unfortunately, many colonists and early settlers decided that Native Americans were "savages" that needed to be "civilized". In fact, Thomas Jefferson, one of the founding fathers, felt that Native Americans could be introduced into a more European way of doing things. He imagined a country where Native Americans didn't live as a separate people, but who rather became a part of American society. He even had a plan for "civilizing" them. He said:

> "The plan of civilizing the Indians is undoubtedly a great improvement on the ancient and totally ineffectual one of beginning with religious missionaries. Our experience has shown that this must be the last step of the process. The following is what has been successful: 1st, to raise cattle, etc., and thereby acquire a knowledge of the value of property; 2d, arithmetic, to calculate that value; 3d, writing, to keep accounts, and here they begin to enclose farms, and the men labor, the women spin and weave; 4th, to read Aesop's Fables and Robinson Crusoe are their first delight. The Creeks and the Cherokees are advanced thus far, and the Cherokees are now instituting a regular government."

As we see here, there were actually a number of tribes (like the Creeks and the Cherokee) that liked the idea, and who began to model their societies after European standards. Especially in the Southeast United States, there was a group of five principal tribes (called the "five civilized tribes") that began to do things like the Americans did. They had roads, local government, and they even wrote a constitution and many accepted Christianity. They were doing everything exactly the way that the settlers wanted. It looked like Jefferson's dream of uniting the Native Americans with settlers was going to become a reality.

Unfortunately for the Native Americans, however, it just wasn't enough for the settlers. They wanted more. They wanted Native American land.

During the years stretching from 1790 to 1830, the population in states like Georgia multiplied about six times over. This was because a lot of people starting moving there to raise valuable crops like cotton, which grows very well in the humid heat of the Southeast. However, all farmers know that more land means more plants and that more plants means more money. But there was a problem: a lot of the land in Georgia already had owners, so a lot of farms couldn't get any bigger.

Sometime after the war of 1812, the Federal government had begun to set up specific borders for Native American tribes in most parts of the Southeast. Why did they wait until after 1812? Well, up until that point, the colonists and early Americans had needed the help of Native Americans to fight foreign powers (like Britain, Spain, and France. However, after the last major battle, the War of 1812, some people in the American government felt that they no longer had to be nice to the Native Americans. Why not? Well, now that everyone had settled down after all of the wars, they felt that they didn't need the help of the Native Americans anymore. Instead of being helpful friends, now they were just annoying neighbors.

So, the government decided to start moving Native Americans onto smaller and smaller pieces of land. Although they weren't too big, these pieces of land, called "reservations", were very important to the Native Americans, as they were like promises from the government that no one would try to take advantage of them anymore. They would be left in peace, and could live their lives as they wanted.

However, some farmers felt frustrated when they had to settle for a smaller piece of land, while there were thousands and thousands of acres nearby that no one was using to grow anything! Think of all the money that they could be making! Do you know what happened next?

First, greedy state governments began to look at Native American lands with drooling mouths. They thought of all the things they could do with those big trees, those strong rivers, and that fertile soil. So, they began to force many tribes to sign "treaties", or agreements, to give more and more of the land to the settlers and farmers, leaving themselves with less and less. However, things weren't always done so legally.

Some settlers actually began to use Native American land without permission. They began to build farms and plant crops, without asking anyone if they minded. Do you know what that's called? It's called "squatting," and it was and still is against the law. In fact, some states began to actively support greedy settlers and farmers when they took away Native American lands. After all, not even the government saw Native Americans as real people. They were more like animals who were just getting in the way and who kept the settlers from doing what they wanted.

In 1831, the Cherokee nation, residing in Georgia, felt that laws being passed against them were too unfair. They thought that the laws were so harsh that they might actually disappear as a people! In reality, this wasn't too far from the truth. The fact is that the people in power, specifically those in the local Georgia government, had begun to make some really mean laws, and the Cherokee were afraid for their lives. They went all the way to the Supreme Court to look for help, but in so many words, the Supreme Court told them: you are nobody. You do not have the legal standing to sue anyone, and you cannot complain about what the government does to you. They even compared Native Americans with little children that the Federal government had to take care of!

Can you imagine that? Here the Native Americans were losing their lands, their inheritance was being stolen, and they were told that they couldn't do anything about it. Upon seeing the decision taken by Chief Justice John Marshall and the Supreme Court against the Native Americans in 1831, President Andrew Jackson said: "John Marshall has made his decision; now let him enforce it! ... Build a fire under them (Native Americans). When it gets hot enough, they'll go".

Wow! The President of the [...] Do you think that it was right of him to speak about Native A[...] at he disliked Native Americans so much? Let's find out more.

PROBLEM 3: ANDREW [...] UNITED STATES FROM 1829-1837, WAS VERY BIASE[...] ECAUSE OF HIS

A painting of President Andrew Jackson

_____

Before he was eventually being promoted to the rmy had enemies on all sides, so entually led some Native Americ larger, ongoing War of 1812 w t of the United States once and rida, and eventually

won several bloody wars. One of the treaties involved the Native Americans losing a huge piece of land.

Jackson accepting the surrender of a Native American leader

Years later, when Andrew Jackson became President of the United States, how do you think he treated the Native Americans? Was he nicer to them, taking steps with his new authority to make lasting peace? No. In fact, the exact opposite happened. After the above court case was passed, Andrew Jackson began to enforce a law that had been passed the year before, called the Indian Removal Act of 1830. This law gave the government permission to buy land from Native Americans, but it *did not* give them permission to *force* them to leave. However, Andrew Jackson, ignoring the spirit of the law, used a great deal of pressure to make the "five civilized tribes" leave their lands in the Southeast United States.

As you can see, it was not easy to be a Native American in those times. They were being attacked in three different ways, and the result was that they had to walk the Trail of Tears.

Chapter 2
Why did the five tribes have to walk on the Trail of Tears?

As we already mentioned, there was a new law in place since 1830 that gave the Federal government permission to negotiate with Native Americans in order to get their lands. The idea was for Native Americans to consider the economic and personal benefits of moving to a new land and getting a fresh start. In fact, the government even set aside a large area of land on the other side of the Mississippi River 9in present day Oklahoma) and called it "Indian Territory", just to encourage Native Americans to move there.

It looked like the Native Americans would finally have a choice. Some could stay, some could go, but it would be each tribe's choice.

Well, that's what was *supposed* to happen. But, that's not what *actually* happened.

As we mentioned, each tribe would be able to make a choice: to stay or to go. For the majority of Native Americans, it wasn't anything that they had to think about. After all, their tribes had been on these lands for thousands of years, and they didn't have the desire to go anywhere. So, most tribes chose to stay.

However, some Native Americans from among these tribes started to do some pretty sneaky stuff. For example, some would claim to be official representatives of their tribe, and they would go to the government and say: "Hi, I'm here representing my people, and we want to sell our land to you!" The government would be happy, and they would prepare and sign a treaty almost right away. However, when they later found out that the whole tribe did not actually want to move, guess what happened? The government made the whole tribe move anyway.

Let's look at an example. In Georgia, there was a gold rush, but a lot of the land where the gold was already belonged to the Cherokee tribe. Their ancestral lands were there, and the majority (over 18,000 Native Americans) did not want to leave. Even when a few within the Cherokee political system tried to sign a favorable treaty with the United States (before squatters and settlers stole everything anyway) the nation as a whole was so offended by this that they threatened to remove those politicians from their posts.

However, these Cherokee politicians eventually went and formed their own political party, called the Treaty Party. Led by a man named Major Ridge, a small group of Cherokees (less than 500) met together one day and approved a treaty (signed by 21 of those present), giving up all Cherokee land east of the Mississippi. Even though the Principal Chief John Ross and thousands of others cried out that the treaty was a fake and that most Cherokee did not want to move, Andrew Jackson's successor, President Martin van Buren, ended up sending in the military and forcing the Native Americans to leave their lands at gunpoint.

What do you think? Was it right of the government to force people to leave their homes because of a lie? What would you have done if you had been there?

Chapter 3
What happened during the Trail of Tears?

As we have seen, this whole period of time is what we call a "dark chapter" of American history. It was a time when people looked at each other only because of the color of their skin. They felt that only some people should be listened to. It was a time when everything that you had could be taken away from you, and there was no one to help you, not even the President of the United States.

When Andrew Jackson, and later Martin Van Buren, decided to enforce the Indian Removal Act of 1830, they were basically forcing the five Native American tribes to leave their lands, most against their will. Let's have a look at each tribe that walked on the Trail of Tears and see what it was like for them.

Here is a list of the tribes and the year in which they had to walk on the Trail:

1. 1831- Choctaw
2. 1832- Seminole
3. 1834- Creek
4. 1837- Chickasaw
5. 1838- Cherokee

Let's look at each tribe one by one to see what happened, and what it was like when they walked the Trail of Tears.

1831- Choctaw Tribe

The first tribe to be moved under the Indian Removal Act was the Choctaw, who lived in what we now call the deep south of the U.S., which included parts of the states of Alabama, Arkansas, Mississippi, and Louisiana. The tribe had signed a series of treaties with the U.S. government, each one taking away a piece of their land. Looking at how the world around them was changing, the Choctaw volunteered to meet with Andrew Jackson's representatives and sign the treaty. A special addition was made stating that any Native Americans who wished to stay behind as American Citizens could do so.

In exchange for 11 million acres, the Choctaw received 15 million in Oklahoma. The treaty was called The Treaty of Dancing Rabbit, and was signed on September 27, 1830.

The Choctaw moved out in three stages, beginning in the fall of 1831. The first group had the most difficult time getting settled in their new land, but it went well for the other two. In fact, Andrew Jackson hoped that the experience would serve as a model for the other tribes who had yet to sign treaties.

Does that mean that there were no problems at all? No. Remember, the roads that the Native Americans walked are called the Trail of Tears. Why? Well, the Arkansas Gazette, a newspaper back then, quoted on Choctaw Chief describing the road as a "trail of tears and death." Why did he say this?

Have a look at the numbers.

About 15,000 Choctaw left on the Trail of Tears, making the slow journey with all of their possessions to Indian Territory in Oklahoma. However, along the way, about 2,500 died. Think about that for a minute. 2,500 people died making the journey. Can you imagine the sadness of the mothers crying for their babies, the friendships that were broken, and the children that ended up as orphans?

Why did so many Choctaw die? The main problems had to do with a lack of food, disease, and being exposed to the cold weather. Travelling during winter in those days wasn't easy. After all, the people had to make their own fires, and look for a warm place to sleep (some towns wouldn't even let the Native Americans stay in their hotels, and they made them sleep outside in the snow!).

The Choctaw finally arrived in Indian Territory a few months later, but what a high price they had paid!

1832- Seminole Tribe

In the distant past, the Seminole people had once been a part of the Creek tribe. However, after they separated, they decided to settle in Florida. Remember the fights during the War of 1812 that Andrew Jackson had fought in? Some of them were against Native Americans from the Seminole tribe, and back then, Andrew Jackson had actually had his eye on acquiring Florida (from Spain) for the U.S. Now, with the Indian Removal Act, Andrew Jackson seemed more determined than ever to get Florida lands for the exclusive use of white American settlers and farmers.

Representatives of the Seminole tribe were called to a meeting in Florida in 1832 to discuss the terms of a possible treaty. It was decided that seven chiefs would go to examine the land west of the Mississippi to see if it was acceptable. While there, they signed an agreement on March 28, 1833, saying that the land was acceptable, essentially agreeing to the treaty with the Federal government and committing their tribe to move. However, when they returned to Florida, most of the chiefs said that the statement was false, that they had been forced to sign, or that they really didn't have any power to represent the rest of the tribe!

None of that mattered to the U.S. government. They had a signed piece of paper, and that was enough for them. Some villages were persuaded to leave, but other refused, and even attacked soldiers stationed nearby.

What happened next was a ten year war, with a cost of over $20 million (almost $500 million today). Most of the Seminole were forcibly removed, although some went deep into the swampland to hide, where they still live today.

1834- Creek Tribe

During the War of 1812, the Creek tribe of Native Americans had a sort of civil war, a war where two sides of the same nation fight against each other. One side wanted to return to more traditional roots, and the other wanted to keep progressing to be more like their American neighbors. Eventually, one of these sides, known as the Red Sticks, began to actively fight against the Americans, while the other side stayed loyal to the United States. When the war was over, Andrew Jackson, commander of the Army that fought the Red Sticks, punished the entire Creek tribe for the actions of a few. According to one historian:

> "Jackson opened this first peace session by faintly acknowledging the help of the friendly Creeks. That done, he turned to the Red Sticks and admonished them for listening to evil counsel. For their crime, he said, the entire Creek Nation must pay. He demanded the equivalent of all expenses incurred by the United States in prosecuting the war, which by his calculation came to 23,000,000 acres (93,000 km2) of land."

Can you believe that? The innocent Creek people, who were living in Alabama and Georgia, lost 23 million acres of land because Andrew Jackson didn't like what a few of their tribe had done! Do you think that was fair? Do you think the police should take you to jail if your neighbor commits a crime?

As time went by, a few members of the Creek nation signed other treaties, which gave more and more land to the U.S. government. Other members of the tribe protested, so a new agreement was signed. On March 24, 1832, the Treaty of Cusseta was signed. This agreement was unique in that it divided up the tribe's land among those living there, and gave each person the opportunity to decide what to do with it. They could either: stay and become a U.S. citizen; or they could exchange their land for some other on the other side of the Mississippi and for some money to get settled. What would you have done?

Many chose to sell, however settlers often took advantage of them and gave them very little money for their land. Others decided to stay, but the locals didn't like that very much. In fact, so many settlers started to use Creek land without permission that a small war even broke out, making the Federal government get involved. Instead of helping the Creeks, who had a signed a treaty guaranteeing them land ownership, the soldiers rounded up the Native Americans and made them walk the Trail of Tears all the way to Indian Territory.

Do you think that the soldiers should have helped the Creeks or the settlers? Who had the real right to live on that land?

1837- Chickasaw Tribe

The Chickasaw tribe was the same one that had fought with Hernando de Soto and his men when they arrived so many years ago. As the years passed, they remained in their lands in the northern part of Mississippi.

After the Indian Removal Act was passed, they were offered land in Indian Territory like the other tribes, but the Chickasaw were worried about being taken advantage of, as they had seen happen to the Creeks and Seminoles before them. Thinking about the future of their people, the Chickasaw decided that the best option would be to give up their land for money, not for more land.

The U.S. government finally agreed, and the Chickasaw bought some land in Indian Territory from the Choctaw tribe. However, it took the U.S. over 30 years to finally pay the Chickasaw. Three thousand Chickasaw made the journey on the Trail of Tears, but over 500 died along the way because of disease (smallpox and dysentery).

Once they arrived on the other side of the Mississippi, the Chickasaw ended up merging with the Choctaw people, essentially dissolving them as an independent tribe for some time.

1838- Cherokee Tribe

As was mentioned previously, one of the saddest tales from this era comes from the Cherokee tribe. The Cherokee were a tribe who lived primarily in modern-day Georgia. In 1835, just before their forced removal, a United States census showed that there were 16,542 Cherokees living in the region. They lived peacefully, but the locals in Georgia had other ideas of what should be done with the land.

Sometime before all this, back in 1802, the Federal government had signed what was called The Compact of 1802 with the state of Georgia. In this agreement, Georgia gave up some of its land to form two new states (Alabama and Mississippi), and the Federal government promised to get rid of the Native Americans that remained on Georgia's land. As the years passed, and Georgia's population grew, the Georgia state government began to take more and more aggressive action against the Cherokee people, believing that they had no right to be in Georgia, and that the Federal government would back them up.

Unlike the Seminole people, the Cherokee never picked up weapons to defend themselves. Rather, under their principal Chief John Ross (Cherokee name *Guwisguwi*) the Cherokees took legal action to defend themselves. In October of 1835, John Ross went to Washington D.C. with some other tribal leaders to protest the constant interference from Georgia militia, who had gone so far as to kidnap John Ross in order to threaten him and his people.

When Chief John Ross and the others were in Washington D.C. fighting for the rights of the Cherokee people, something really sneaky happened. A U.S. agent got together some Cherokees (led by a Native American named Major Ridge) who felt differently, and got them to sign a treaty in December, promising to give the Federal government all Cherokee lands!

Of course, this document was no good and did not represent what the Cherokee people really wanted. Remember, the U.S. government could not technically "force" anyone to leave their land; it had to be the choice of the Native American tribe. However, the U.S. senate approved this treaty on May 23, 1836, and gave the Cherokee people two years to leave their ancestral lands.

Do you think that the U.S. senators should have approved a treaty that was obviously false? What should the Cherokee have done? Should they have picked up their guns and fought like the Seminole, or should they just pack up their bags and go? What would you have done if you had been a part of the Cherokee nation?

Some groups, mostly those who were part of Major Ridge's opposition group, accepted government money and willingly left before the two year "grace period" had ended. However, most Cherokee stayed behind to protest what was obviously an illegal action. They had a right to stay on the land of their forefathers, and no one should be able to take them away.

Many white Americans even wrote to the President, begging him not to take action against the Cherokee. However, he did not listen. On May 17, 1838, 7,000 soldiers arrived in the capital of the Cherokee tribe and began to round up the people ten days later. During the next three weeks, the entire Cherokee nation, men, women, and children, were forced from their homes, often at gunpoint, and sent to live in temporary holding camps.

In these camps, there was disease everywhere, and there wasn't enough food to eat. Can you imagine soldiers coming to your house one day, and making you leave it behind? Can you imagine looking around you and seeing all of your neighbors forced to walk in the streets, many crying, and then to be locked up in a jail like a bunch of criminals?

During the entire summer, the Cherokee people lived in these camps, mostly in Tennessee. Over 350 people died from sickness while in these camps.

Chief John Ross, seeing that there was no way they could go back, asked the U.S. government if the Cherokee council (politicians in charge of the Cherokee people) could oversee the removal operation instead. The government agreed, so the Cherokee council organized 12 wagon trains, each with about 1,000 people.

It was now the Cherokee Tribe's turn to walk the trail of tears, the same trail that so many had walked before them.

From October to November, 1838, all of the wagon trains left. By the time that they arrived in Indian Territory in the spring, around 4,000 Cherokee had died and been buried on the way.

What was it like to walk on the Trail of Tears with the Cherokee people? Let's listen to some of their comments. Samuel Cloud was a child when we walked the Trail, only nine years old. He said:

> "I know what it is to hate. I hate those white soldiers who took us from our home. I hate the soldiers who make us keep walking through the snow and ice toward this new home that none of us ever wanted. I hate the people who killed my father and mother. I hate the white people who lined the roads in their woolen clothes that kept them warm, watching us pass. None of those white people are here to say they are sorry that I am alone. None of them care about me or my people. All they ever saw was the color of our skin. All I see is the color of theirs and I hate them."

One soldier who had participated in the initial rounding up the Cherokee people, John G Burnett, wrote:

> "The removal of Cherokee Indians from their life long homes in the year of 1838 found me a young man in the prime of life and a Private soldier in the American Army…I was sent as interpreter into the Smoky Mountain Country in May, 1838, and witnessed the execution of the most brutal order in the History of American Warfare. I saw the helpless Cherokees arrested and dragged from their homes, and driven at the bayonet point into the stockades…Children were often separated from their parents."

This was a very dark time in American history. This was a time when the color of your skin was all that mattered.

The Cherokee people arrived in Indian Territory in 1839, the last to walk the Trail of Tears.

Chapter 4
What was it like to be a kid during this time?

To be a kid during these times, you would have found yourself in one of two situations: either the white child of a settler or the Native American child of one the "Five Civilized Tribes". Let's see what it was like to be a kid in both situations.

The White Child of a Settler

Imagine that you were born somewhere in the Southeast United States. Your dad is probably a farmer and your mom takes care of things in the house. You go to school in a large, one-room building with kids of all ages. After school, you like to explore the woods near your house and just hang out with your friends.

Now, you have seen Native Americans in town. They sometimes buy from the same stores that your parents do, and you may have seen Native American children when you go out for your walks. What do you think? Would you be afraid of them? After all, although they speak some English, they also might speak a different language then you. Some of the boys might have long hair, and they might dress differently than you do.

Now, imagine that, in your house, your father starts to talk about how "the Indians are keeping us from growing" and that "they won't give us what's rightfully ours". Wouldn't you be a little confused? Of course, it's not always easy to understand complicated things like treaties, compacts, and tribal history. But even as a kid, you would probably be able to see that something unfair was happening to the Native American tribes. Would you have stood up for them and told your parents what you thought?

The Child of a Native American

Now, imagine the other side. Imagine that you had been born as a Native American, surrounded by white settlers who wanted to take your family's land. What would you have thought when, as you played with your friends in the woods, you saw a group of white kids looking at you? Would you have been scared that they were going to throw rocks at you or treat you badly? Would you have gone to speak with them, to try to make friends, or would you have been mean to them.

Back in your house, you may have heard you parents talk about "the white Americans who want to take away our sacred lands" and "who don't understand us or see us as equals." Even as a kid, you know that you are equal to other people, just as important as a white kod. You know that you are the same as everyone else, so how do you think it felt to be treated differently just because your skin wasn't white?

When the soldiers came in with their guns to take you away from your house and to make you walk thousands of miles to a new land, where you would have to start over, would you have fought back? What would you have done to make sure that you didn't get separated from your family along the way? And what would you have done if your brother, sister, mother, or father had gotten sick, and there was no medicine?

What would you have thought of white people after having walked the Trail of Tears?

It wasn't easy to be a kid in those days. You would have had to suffer a lot as a Native American kid, and you would have had to stand up for what was right as a white kid. Even though the adults might not have listened, it would have been the right thing to do.

Chapter 5
How did it end?

For most Native Americans, their experience with the Trail of Tears ended when they arrived in Indian Territory. There, they had to build homes, start farming, and try to keep on living. However, some Native Americans chose to stay in their lands. Even though many had the legal right to do so, it wasn't always easy to stay. What was it like for them? Let's see an example.

About 15,000 Choctaw people walked the Trail of Tears from 1831 to 1833. However, using the legal rights given to them in the Treaty of Dancing Rabbit Creek, about 5,000 to 6,000 decided to remain legally on their lands and become American citizens. This decision was not popular among the locals, who desperately wanted their land. What was it like for the Choctaw who remained behind?

In 1849, they described their life:

> "We have had our habitations torn down and burned, our fences destroyed, cattle turned into our fields and we ourselves have been scourged, manacled, fettered and otherwise personally abused, until by such treatment some of our best men have died."

Did you see how their neighbors treated them? Although they were legal U.S. citizens, landowners, and families, they were treated like criminals and, in some cases, like animal. It was not easy for those who remained behind and who decided not to walk the Trail of Tears.

When all of the tribes from the Southeast United States had walked on the trail, the largest part of the "Indian Removal" was accomplished. Settlers moved into the abandoned lands and began to cultivate large quantities of cash crops like tobacco and cotton. They made more money, bought more slaves, and were very happy and wealthy all the way until the American Civil War broke out about thirty years later.

What happened after the Native Americans walked the Trail of Tears?

The forced removal of Native American tribes from the Southeast United States would forever change the way that people looked at Native Americans. Unfortunately, many settlers looked at Native Americans as less than human, and as people with no rights or dignity. Making the Native Americans walk the Trail of Tears had confirmed all that, and it made sure that white settlers would continue to harass and take advantage of Native Americans. Let's see some examples.

As white settlers continued to push west, exercising their "Manifest Destiny", they eventually crossed the Mississippi River. And guess who they ran into? That's right; they ran smack dab into the same Native Americans that they had forcibly removed earlier. What do you think happened next? The white settlers again began to harass the Native Americans living in Indian Territory, forcing them to, again, give up more and more of their land.

In 1889, President Grover Cleveland signed an act, part of a group of acts called the Indian Appropriation Acts that permitted white settlers to enter "unassigned" lands and claim them for themselves. This further limited the land available to Native Americans.

A series of treaties and agreements eventually led to the formation of the state of Oklahoma in 1907, when Indian Territory officially ceased to exist. The Native Americans were finally placed into smaller reservations of land, where they continue today.

Conclusion

On July 4, 1776, a group of Patriots gathered together in Philadelphia and prepared the wording of the Declaration of Independence, a step that would eventually lead to the formation of the United States government. Look at the second sentence from that Declaration:

> "We hold these truths to be self-evident, that all men are created equal, that they are endowed by their Creator with certain unalienable Rights, that among these are Life, Liberty and the pursuit of Happiness."

Those are beautiful words, aren't they? These words meant that the United States of America, from its very beginning, would be a place where men and women of all sorts, no matter what color they were, could come here and expect to be treated with dignity and respect. They would be equals with everyone.

After reading this handbook, what do you think? Do you think that President Andrew Jackson treated Native Americans as equals? Do you think that the white settlers who tried to take land from their Native American neighbors were respecting their rights? Do you think that the people who walked the Trail of Tears were treated as human being who could enjoy Life, Liberty, and the Pursuit of Happiness?

The answer, of course, is no. When the United States government forced Native Americans to leave their homes and march far away to a distant land, they were not treating them as equals; they were treating them like animals. That bad treatment continued on for many years to come.

As white settlers pushed further and further west, eventually reaching the Pacific Ocean, they had more and more fights with Native Americans. And, sadly, the Native Americans had no one who would help them.

For example, in 1860, a tribe of Native Americans called the Wiyot were living peacefully on an island off the California coast. One night, on February 26, a group of white men went out to that island and killed everyone they could find- from man to little baby- over 200 people. What did local law enforcement do? Nothing. What did the Army do? Nothing. What did the President do upon seeing that 200 innocent people had been murdered?

Nothing at all.

When Native Americans walked the Trail of Tears, they left behind the only home that they had ever known. But more than that, they also left behind a world where they were viewed as equals. From that moment on, and for many years to come, Native Americans would be persecuted everywhere that they went, and no one would help them.

Many years later, in 1987, the United States government officially recognized the suffering of the innocent Native Americans, and established a National Park dedicated to remembering the Trail of Tears. Every year, descendants of those who walked it get together to commemorate what their ancestors did and to talk about it.

Now that so many years have passed, do you think that we have learned any lessons from the past? Well, it's true that the government isn't forcing Native Americans to move around anymore, but do you think that everyone in the United States today is treated equally, like the Declaration of Independence wanted? Do you think that the color of our skin doesn't matter anymore, and that Native Americans, Blacks, White, Latinos, Jews, Italians, Russians, Albanians, and people from the Middle East are all living together happily today, or is there still room for improvement?

The Trail of Tears has taught us what can happen when we ignore the suffering of others, or when we try to take advantage of people who are different than us. An important lesson is to realize that, no matter how someone looks or how someone worships, they are still a human who is worthy of our respect.

What do you think? Are you brave enough to treat others with dignity, or will you make them walk a Trail of Tears?

The choice is yours.

The Pony Express

Introduction

Billy squinted his eyes a little in order to be able to see the road ahead in the darkness. His horse was galloping at a steady pace, and Billy himself felt pretty good. He had mounted the horse a few miles back, but something in the air wasn't quite right. There was no moon out, and some low clouds were covering the stars completely. Both Billy and the horse knew the way to the next station well enough, so he wasn't worried about getting lost or anything. But, as he rode along the path he knew so well, Billy was sure of one thing: *he wasn't alone.*

Even his horse was acting a little strangely, like it was afraid of something. The air was crisp here in Nevada, and the only sounds he could hear were the hoof beats of his steed. He had heard that this part of the route was dangerous, and that the local Native American tribe, the Paiute people, had just come out of a particularly difficult winter. Settlers in the area had been competing with the Paiute people for land and for natural resources. After a tough winter and an almost constant lack of food, the Paiute people had teamed up with two other tribes that lived nearby to wage war on the United States of America and on all of its citizens. Settlers and soldiers were all part of the war, in their eyes, but there was one group of people that represented everything they hated about the American way of doing things: the riders of the Pony Express.

Billy knew that, as he rode through the chilly Nevada night in May of 1860, any Paiute warriors who were watching the roads would be sure to hear him coming and would view it as a special privilege to kill him. After all, the riders of the Pony Express weren't easy targets.

Pulling his revolver from his holster, Billy leaned down closer to his horse to make himself a smaller target. The Native Americans might not respect him, but they respected his horse and knew how valuable it was. They would shoot their arrows high to avoid hitting it. Billy just hoped that luck was with him tonight.

As he rode towards the next stop on his route, about halfway before he could change places with another rider and get some sleep before riding back in the opposite direction, he heard some movement in the bushes beside him. Without waiting to see what it was, he yelled at his horse and nudged his spurs into its side. The horse ran faster than a minnow can swim a dipper, but, for a few moments, it looked like it might not be fast enough. Three Paiute braves came out into the road behind him, each one pulling an arrow back on his bow. He ducked as two arrows went flying over his head, and he said a silent prayer. It wasn't long before the danger was behind him. A few miles down the road, he honked the horn he carried with him to alert the attendant to prepare another horse.

Once he arrived, Billy jumped off his horse and turned back around to lift off the mochila, or mail bag, that he had been sitting on. By the light of the oil lamp burning near the stable, Billy could see something sticking out of the thick leather. An arrow. He pulled it out and threw it onto the ground. He had no time to worry about that now: he had to be back on the road in less than a minute, and the next horse was already waiting for him.

With his mochila over his shoulder, Billy jogged to the next horse and got ready for the next stage of his ride. Smiling to himself, he stepped into the stirrup and swung his thin frame over the horse and into the saddle. Without a word, he left the station attendant behind and raced into the night. His life was an adventure, and, arrows or no arrows, he loved every minute of it.

Have you ever heard of the Pony Express before? Do you know why young men like Billy were willing to risk their lives and ride in the dead of night to deliver mail? Do you know if anyone famous was ever part of the Pony Express?

In this handbook, we are going to learn all about this famous mail carrying service. We will see what it was like to ride the long trail from St. Joseph, Missouri to Sacramento, California alongside the Pony Express. What exciting things can you expect to learn?

First, we will learn what led up to the Pony Express. For example, how did so many people end up living in California during the mid-1800s? What were the other options for sending letters and small packages? Then, in the next section, we will see why the Pony Express was so necessary, and why it provided a service that no one else could at the time. We will see why whoever supplied the communication lines could make a difference in history.

The next section will be tremendously exciting as we will see how the Pony Express was started and what some of the biggest challenges were. Did you know that the Pony Express looked to hire young men who were orphans? Do you know why? We will find out. We will see the route that they travelled and see why these riders had to be fearless to do their job. Then, the next section will give you a chance to see what it was like to be a kid back then. You will climb into the saddle and ride along with the Pony Express over mountains and across rivers to get the mail to its destination on time.

After that, we will see a little more about how the Pony Express ended. Even though it was a particularly special arrangement, the world changed quickly and soon no one needed the Pony Express anymore. Then, we will find out what happened after.

Are you ready to start learning? Then grab your hat and let's go ride on the Pony Express!

Chapter 1: What Led Up to the Pony Express?

The Pony Express was established as a rapid courier service between the East and the West, from St. Joseph Missouri to Sacramento, California. There were tens of thousands of people living and working in California that wanted news of what was happening in the East and who wanted to send letters and packages to friends, family members, and business partners living back east. But you may wonder: why did all those people move so far away from their friends and families back east in the first place? Why were they in California? Let's learn the answers.

As you may know, California did not always belong to the United States. Although different countries looked at owning a piece of the Pacific Coast for a long time, it was Spain who actually was the first to build permanent settlements as far north as the San Francisco Bay. The Spanish remained in control of California until 1821, when the local residents (the Mexican people) rebelled against Spain and gained their independence.

The land then came under Mexican control until 1846. During that time, more and more American settlers began to arrive and to raise crops, graze their livestock, and establish trading routes with the East. The settlers stayed mainly in the north while the Spanish-speaking Mexican citizens (called *Californios*) stayed in the south. Although the two groups didn't actually like each other, California was large enough so that there was plenty of space between them and there weren't any serious problems. However, all of that changed on May 13, 1846, when the United States declared war on Mexico. After admitting Texas to the Union, a dispute with Mexico over the exact border between Texas and Mexico led to fighting among soldiers and eventually to a large war. The war ended on February 2, 1848, when the Treaty of Guadalupe Hidalgo was signed to end the war, and many lands, including California, were given to the United States.

Small groups of settlers started to move west, but in January of 1848, that small trickle of people going to California turned into a raging river when gold was discovered. Within a short time, some 300,000 people had moved to California to seek riches, and a lot of them were successful. Whole towns were built almost overnight, but people who moved to California didn't want to lose touch with the ones they behind. As a result, they were desperate to have communication with the outside world.

There were several ways of getting communication to the people living in the west, but none of them were fast, and they weren't always reliable. For example, some people sent their mail and packages by stagecoach. Do you know what a stagecoach is? Look at the picture below.

Stagecoaches (like the one in the picture) went all over the Old West, carrying precious packages and letters to those who wanted them. However, do you know what the biggest problem with stagecoaches was? It could take around 24 days for the letter to reach its destination! And that wasn't even the worst of it. If someone were to send a letter or package by boat, it could have taken over a month! Think of waiting one month for a letter, for a reply to an important question, or to hear news.

If that seems almost unbelievable, think about the Mexican-American War that we mentioned earlier, the one that ended with the signing of the Treaty of Guadalupe Hidalgo. Even though war against Mexico was declared on May 13, 1846, the people living in California didn't find out officially for *two months!* Can you imagine that? The country was at war with California's next-door neighbor, but they didn't even know it!

As more and more people moved to the West, the need to have fast and reliable communication with the East became more critical than ever. The railroad still had a long way to go before it reached the Pacific Coast, and telegraph lines hadn't yet been approved for construction. Whoever could find a way to help people on opposite sides of the country communicate quickly with each other would become rich and famous and would help a lot of people along the way.

In 1860, three men came up with the perfect solution to the communication problem.

Chapter 2: Why Did the Pony Express Happen?

How relevant is communication in your life? Take a moment to think about how many people you communicate with every day. Be sure to include conversations, notes, text messages, phone calls, emails, and even status updates, tweets, and posts on social networks. Do you think you communicate with five people a day? Ten? Thirty? Fifty? More? Communication is important to all of us because it lets us be a part of the lives of the people we love, of our friends and families. Communication also lets us know what's happening around the world and lets us run our businesses. Now, imagine if you had to wait days or weeks to get a response to each message you sent out? How would you feel?

Back in the Old West, before there were telephone and telegraph lines put up everywhere, people had to wait weeks or even months for news to travel from one side of the country to the other. You can imagine how excited they were to get a letter or a note from someone they loved. However, communication with the West (and with California especially) became much more influential than simply sending letters or notes- it had to do with the future of the United States.

When California was accepted as a free state into the Union during the Great Compromise of 1850, the goal was to ease the growing tensions between the slave states and the non-slave states. For a time, there was even some talk of dividing California into two states, Northern and Southern, but that never happened. After California became a state in 1850, it became an indispensable place that both the Confederate States and the Union wanted on their side if a war were to break out. What made California so desirable to both sides, especially taking into consideration the nearness of Civil War? Let's find out.

First, there was the issue of **politics**. There could be no doubt that a Civil War was coming- everybody could feel it in the air. The question was: which state would be on which side? Even though California has joined the Union as a free state, there was nothing stopping the people living there from changing their minds later and joining the Southern cause. In fact, there was even a pretty good-sized group of people living in California that wanted to have slavery and support the Confederates! As a result of such politics, there was a lot of interest in establishing and maintaining good communication with the West.

Another reason that so many people were interested in communicating with California and the West had to do with the **gold** that was being mined there. Whoever had California as a friend could be sure that they would get lots of financial help before, during, and after a war. And gold didn't just mean wealth- it meant power and having the best and latest technology. Later on, we will see what this all meant for the side who finally got to be friend with California.

Finally, everyone looked at the **large population** of the West. With some many tens of thousands of people who had moved there, each one of those people represented a vote that could either help or hurt the people in Washington. They represented potential soldiers for an army, workers in new industries, and business leaders to help the national economy. Communication with those people would ensure the strength of the entire nation and would make them a powerful friend to either the North or the South during the future Civil War.

Thus, to make sure that California would be friendly to their cause, one side or the other would have to promote regular communication with the people in charge there, including the politicians and the businessmen. Communication with the Old West became more valuable than simply sending letters back and forth; it became a fight for the very future of the United States. But what could the solution be?

Stagecoaches took too long and had problems from hostile Native Americans and robbers along the way and boats took even longer.

Telegraph lines had been put up in key routes in the Eastern United States, but they only went as far west as St. Joseph, and no one from the government had offered money to put them even further west yet. In the meantime, a war was about to happen, and everyone wanted California to be on their side. Who could come up with a solution to this difficult problem?

Chapter 3: What Happened During the Days of the Pony Express?

Three American businessmen loyal to the Union saw a significant opportunity when they looked at the communication situation between the eastern United States and the West. These men, William H. Russell, William B. Waddle and Alexander Majors were already involved in the shipping business, working primarily with stagecoaches. However, they saw an opportunity to fill a gap in the communication systems that existed back then. They thought that they could find a faster way of transporting letters and small packages from the East to the West. If they were successful, they could help people stay in touch with loved ones, help tie California to the Union, and they could also get rich. What was their plan? They would use small horses and devoted riders as a fast delivery system.

What would the advantages be of using horses and riders instead of a stagecoach? Stagecoaches weighed more because they carried passengers and cargo. Sometimes, stagecoaches got stuck in the mud and the sand, and it took time to get them out. The horses got tired and needed to rest, and the roads weren't so great for the large wagons. However, one man riding on a horse could travel at about twice the speed of a stagecoach without the need to take frequent rests. However, the distance from St. Joseph to Sacramento was about 1,900 miles. No horse could ride that far without getting tired, and no rider could either. So, then, what was the solution?

The solution would be to have a series of horse stables built along the route about every ten miles or so. Each horse would travel at a moderately-paced gallop (about 10-15 miles per hour) for one "stage" of ten miles. As the rider got near the next stable, called a stationhouse, he would honk his horn or yell to let the attendant know that he needed to get another horse ready. When the rider arrived, another well-rested horse would be there to greet him. All he would have to do would be to throw his little mailbag into the saddle and take off again, letting the previous horse rest for a while. He would do this for about eight to ten hours, and cover between 75 and 100 miles. Then, another rider would take his mail bag and a fresh horse and keep riding. The tired rider would rest at the stationhouse for about eight hours before waking up to ride with some more mail back in the opposite direction, back where he came from.

The idea was genius! After all, instead of having to wait three or four weeks to get their mail and pertinent letters from St. Joseph, people in the West could now get what they needed in only nine or ten days! Can you understand why so many people got excited when they heard about the Pony Express? But now that the three men had the brilliant idea for the Pony Express, how would they make it happen? It took a lot of money and a lot of planning. They had to make a route, buy some horses, hire some riders, and then get some customers. Let's look at each of these things to see how the Pony Express dream became a reality.

Making the route. The first step towards establishing the Pony Express was deciding what route it would take. The most crucial decision was to decide what two cities would be on either end of the trail. The cities would have to be large and full of people who wanted to send correspondence to the other side of the country. The town of St. Joseph, Missouri was on the furthest western border of the state and would reduce the riding time instead of leaving from St. Louis or Kansas City.

St. Joseph had a telegraph line and could receive urgent message from cities like Boston, New York City, and Washington D.C. The messages could be quickly written down and carried by Pony Express to the intended recipient in a matter of days.

However, which city should be the one on the other side of the trail? Although most of the businessmen and people who wanted to use the service lived in San Francisco and Oakland, it was decided that Sacramento would be the city that the riders took the mail to. Why was Sacramento chosen? Well, from Sacramento, there were large boats (called ferries) that could take the mail the rest of the way to the Bay area (where San Francisco and Oakland were). That way, the new mail could be picked up, and the riders could start their journey eastward again.

So the two principal cities had been chosen: St. Joseph, Missouri on the eastern end and Sacramento, California on the Western end. A distance of some 1,900 miles separated the two cities. Which would be the best way to cross the plains and the mountains to get there? It was decided to follow the Oregon Trail west as far as Wyoming Territory. From there, the riders would head southwest across Utah and the Nevada Desert, climb over the Sierra Nevada Mountains, before heading across the California Central Valley to Sacramento.

The route had been set. Now, they needed horses.

Buying the horses. What kind of horses do you think were bought for this new communication system? Remember the name "Pony Express". A "pony" refers to smaller horses that can run faster over longer distances. In fact, the majority of the horses bought for the Pony Express were only about 4 feet 10 inches tall, weighing about 900 pounds. (For a comparison, the average horse is about 5 feet 6 inches tall and weighs 1,200 pounds).

About 400 horses were bought from all over the West, most for $200 each. There were divided up into groups who lived and were cared for at 184 stations laid out along the Pony Express trail. The horses were well fed and were never worked too hard. They were rested after running ten miles when the rider switched to a new horse.

Now they had the trail and the horses, now they needed the riders. How would they get them?

Hiring the riders. If you were looking for someone to ride a horse along the route of the Pony Express, what kind of a person would you look for? Would his size matter? Would his age matter? What about his family? Have a look at an actual ad made by the Pony Express when they were looking for riders:

Did you see what kind of people the poster says they were looking for? It mentions young, skinny men. In fact, history tells us that none of the riders on the Pony Express weighed more than 110 pounds. Why do you think they wanted men who didn't weight too much? Well, think about this: horses can only carry a certain amount of weight before they tire out and even get injuries. So that means that if the rider weighs less, then the horse can carry more mail, and the company (who charges for the weight of each letter) would make more money. Also, a lighter load meant that the horse would run faster and get the mail to its destination sooner.

Orphans were preferred because of the long distance that the riders would travel. Even though most of the riders weren't orphans, the idea was to have riders who wouldn't be too worried thinking about leaving behind their families. They wanted serious men who would focus on the job. Also, the poster said: "Must…be willing to risk death daily." As you can imagine, a job like that attracted a certain type of person: somebody who was looking for adventure.

One of the founders of the Pony Express, Alexander Majors, was a religious man and asked each of the new riders to take a special oath:

> "I _____ do hereby swear, before the great and living God, that during my engagement, and while I am an employee of Russell, Majors, & Waddell, I will, under no circumstances, use profane language. I will drink no intoxicating liquors; that I will not quarrel or fight with any other employee of the firm, and that in every respect, I will conduct myself honestly, faithful to my duties, and so direct my acts as to win the confidence of my employers. So help me God."[1]

This oath helped the new riders to understand that they were about to start something dead serious. The young men were to act as gentlemen even when riding through the Wild West. Instead of being just another cowboy, they were to represent the best that the American culture had to offer.

What did a pony express rider take with him on his rides? The single most indispensable item was the mochila, or mailbag, as seen in the picture below.

Inside the mochila, up to about 20 pounds worth of mail could be carried. The rider would also take a canteen of water with him, a bible, a revolver for personal protection, and a horn for letting the station attendants know when he was arriving (although many later riders stopped carrying a horn).

Each rider made $25 per week. Was that a lot of money back then? Well, for comparison, the average laborer made only about $1 per week, so you can imagine how happy the riders were every time payday came around!

Several famous cowboys from the Old West got their start riding for the Pony Express, including William Cody (better known as Buffalo Bill). Buffalo Bill was present for every major event in the Old West and Frontier America, including the Gold Rush, the construction of the railroad, and even the Civil War. As a rider for the Pony Express, he once had to ride 322 miles nonstop during 21 hours, using 21 different horses to deliver the mail! Most of the riders were willing to work just as hard. Once the route had been chosen, and the horses and riders had been obtained, the Pony Express only had to find its customers and carry their mail. How did they do so?

Getting the customers. From the very beginning, the founders of the Pony Express knew that their business wouldn't last forever. But until the telegraph and railroad were completed, they knew that they could provide a valuable service for lots of people. Their first hope was to secure a contract with the U.S. Government to be the exclusive (only) carrier of Federal and Army communications. However, when that didn't happen (the contract went to a stagecoach company) the founders decided to focus on private businessmen and wealthy citizens. The price of carrying letters wasn't cheap, so not everyone could afford it. However, to those who had the money and who needed an urgent response to something, the price was worth it. How much did the Pony Express charge for carrying letters across the country? Look at the following quote from one reference work:

---

[1] Quotation source: http://www.blm.gov/ut/st/en/fo/salt_lake/recreation/back_country_byways/pony_express_trail/story_of_the_pony.html

> "The cost to send a 1/2 ounce letter was $5.00 at the beginning [and was] a costly sum in those days and mostly unaffordable to the general public. By the end period of the Pony Express, the price had dropped to $1.00 per 1/2 ounce. Even the $1.00 rate was considered a lot of money ($26 in 2012 U.S. Dollars)."[2]

As you can see, not everyone could use the Pony Express, mainly just the government and rich businesspeople. However, the Pony Express earned a good reputation and only ever lost one mailbag (after an attack by Paiute Native Americans in 1860). How did the Pony Express advertise their services? They got new clients by putting up posters everywhere similar to the one below.

Within a short time, people wanted to see just how good this service was. On April 3, 1860, they got their chance. Look at the following description of what the first ride was like:

> "On April 3, 1860, the first official delivery began at the eastern terminus of the Pony Express in St. Joseph, Missouri. Amid great fanfare and with many dignitaries present, a mail pouch containing 49 letters, five telegrams and miscellaneous papers was handed to a rider. At 7:15 p.m., a cannon was fired and the rider bolted off to a waiting ferry boat.
>
> The Pony Express was set up to provide a fresh horse every 10-15 miles and a fresh rider every 75-100 miles. 75 horses were needed total to make a one-way trip. Average speed was 10 miles per hour. On April 9 at 6:45 p.m., the first rider from the east reached Salt Lake City, Utah. Then, on April 12, the mail pouch reached Carson City, Nevada at 2:30 p.m.
>
> The riders raced over the Sierra Nevada Mountains, through Placerville, California and on to Sacramento. Around midnight on April 14, 1860, the first mail pouch was delivered via the Pony Express to San Francisco."[3]

Can you imagine how exciting it must have been to see the riders leave, to watch them race across the country, and then finally arrive in Sacramento?

The Pony Express dream had become a reality, and everyone was tremendously excited about it.

---

[2] Quotation source: http://en.wikipedia.org/wiki/Pony_Express
[3] Quotation source: http://www.nps.gov/poex/historyculture/history1.htm

Chapter 4: What Was It Like to Be a Kid During the Pony Express?

Can you imagine riding alongside someone like Buffalo Bill as he raced through the Great Plains, the Nevada desert, or over the Sierra Nevada mountains? Can you imagine looking out for hostile Native Americans and trying to ride faster than robbers chasing you? Do you see the surprised looks on the faces of the stagecoach drivers as you go racing past them and leaving them to eat your dust? That would have been a lot of fun!

There is no doubt about it: the riders on the Pony Express led lives of adventure. They were awake and riding at night when the whole world was fast asleep. They rode through the rain, through the snow, and through the hottest days you can imagine. Their missions were so momentous that they didn't stop to speak to anyone on the way. All they thought about was: make it to the next station.

The riders were supposed to get a rest every eight hours or so, after changing horses seven or eight times. However, there were occasions, like the one we saw with Buffalo Bill, when the new riders weren't ready, were sick, or were missing. What would happen then? The young men would have to do the same thing that Buffalo Bill did: keep on riding. Even though they were tired, they would have to keep on riding all the through the next stage. The mail had to be delivered.

Was it always fun and adventure on the Pony Express trail? Unfortunately, things weren't always so enthusiastic. Even though the pay was good and the riders tried to get along with everyone they met, the country was going through some serious problems. Do you remember the problems that many settlers were having with the Paiute Native American tribe? Do you remember what the problem was about?

Try to see things from the perspective of the Paiute people. For generations, they had lived on their land and hunted and raised crops. They had borders with other Native American tribes in the area and their leaders tried terribly hard to keep the peace with everyone. However, as more and more Americans began to cross through their lands, to build houses and farms, and to settle it, they were forced to grow crops in smaller areas, share their hunting grounds with more people, and fight to defend the borders that had been established for so long.

The Paiute tribe, along with other tribes in the area, saw their way of life being threatened. They felt that the only way to stay alive and to stay together as a people was to fight against the settlers and to kill the people who they saw as taking away their land and their freedoms. The Pony Express, because it was always riding through Paiute territory and because it represented Americans expanding westward, became a distinct target. One young man, named, Billy Tate, was only 14 years old when he was killed by some Paiute Native American warriors. He killed seven of his attackers before dying himself. Note how one reference work explains his brave last fight:

> "14-year old Billy Tate is often cited as the bravest pony rider of them all. Delivering mail at the height of a war with the local Indian tribes in the Ruby Valley of Utah, Tate was often pursued, but was able to escape thanks to his horses being able to outrun Indian horses.
>
> Tate's luck finally ran out, when Indians ambushed and surrounded him. Tate fought to the death. Finally falling from his horse, Tate's last act was to grab the mailbag and shield it with his body. As a mark of respect for the young man's courage, the Indians reattached his mailbag to

the saddle, marked it with a sign of inviolability, and let the mustang go. Several hours later, the horse arrived at the nearest settlement alone, bringing the post but not its rider."[4]

Knowing that something so terrible happened to Billy Tate would have made anyone sad. But if you were a rider, would that have made you stop? Of course not; the riders of the Pony Express believed that they had a serious job to do, and they were determined to make sure the mail got to its destination, even if they had to ride hard, fast, and for a long time.

To have been a kid back then would have meant having a life of adventure!

---

[4] Quotation source: http://sixthscaleamericanhistory.yuku.com/topic/1565#.ULd5F6xTxeA

Chapter 5: How Did the Pony Express End?

The Pony Express was an exciting idea, and we already saw the first successful ride on April 3, 1860. For nineteen months, the Pony Express ran twice weekly without any interruptions (with the exception of a few during the Paiute wars). After nineteen months, on October 26, 1861, the Pony Express announced its official closure. What had happened to close this exciting chapter of American history? There were at least three factors: unmet expectations, the telegraph, and the railroad. Let's look at each of them.

Unmet expectations: The Pony Express got people excited because they hoped to receive regular news reports from the East Coast. And while, in some special cases, this did indeed happen (like during the 1860 Presidential Election) in most cases the Pony Express focused on carrying personal communication between people. As a result, many of those living on the West Coast felt a little disappointed and just as cut off as always from current events back east. Also, the price stayed so high that those hoping to use the service could never actually afford it. It was just too expensive for an average person to use (anywhere from one weeks' to one months' worth of wages!)

The founders themselves were disappointed with the financial results of the Pony Express. They had spent about $200,000 to start the business and to keep it running, but only made back $90,000. The high expectations that the founders had for the Pony Express were never fully realized.

Let's look at another reason the Pony Express ended.

The Telegraph. Do you know what the telegraph was? The telegraph, invented in the United States by Samuel Morse and Alfred Vail, was a method of sending electrical signals over long distances. The code, called "Morse Code," would be translated into letters and words. A station on each side would either broadcast or receive the message, writing it down for the recipient. Although it was not as personal as a handwritten letter, the telegraph could transmit key messages instantly over long distances (it would be used during the Civil War to allow Lincoln to direct his troops with up-to-date information). But what did the telegraph have to do with the end of the Pony Express?

Remember, the Pony Express was not for everyday communication; it was only for urgent letters and news. When the telegraph finally reached all the way from the east coast to the west coast, those same fundamental messages could then be sent by telegraph. As a result, the Pony Express was not needed anymore.

This came as a surprise to no one, even to the founders of the Pony Express. However, they had hoped that, in the meantime, they would make more money along the way. The First Transcontinental Telegraph was installed and connected on October 24, 1861, and the Pony Express closed its doors two days later.

The Railroad.

On May 10, 1869, the Transcontinental Railroad, going from San Francisco, California, all the way to New York City on the East Coast was completed. Now, large steam trains carrying cargo, passengers, and correspondence could travel from one side of the country to the other quickly. How quickly?

While a ship would take several weeks to make the journey coast to coast (going around the tip of South America) and taking a wagon would have lasted several months, one train that left New York City on June 4, 1876 arrived in San Francisco just 83 hours and 39 minutes later. In other words, the people crossed the country in only about three and a half days! That is even faster than the Pony Express could ever have hoped to travel.

Even though the Pony Express was a terrific idea and it did its job exceedingly well for nineteen months, technology kept improving, and eventually the new technology could do things that the Pony Express riders and even stagecoaches never could. The train didn't have to worry about thieves, about Native American attacks, about horses getting tired, or even about too much rain. The train could run 24 hours a day, as long as there was enough fuel, and could carry thousands and thousands of pounds of letters, not just one bag full.

In the quickly changing United States, especially after the Civil War, urgent messages were sent by telegraph and letters and correspondence were sent by train. The world had changed, and the Pony Express had finished its job.

After the Civil War, the remaining horses and materials from the Pony Express were sold to Wells Fargo. Wells Fargo was a stagecoach company that served the little tows far away from the train stations that still needed stagecoaches to move people and goods around. However, even Wells Fargo would have to change their job as the trains and then roads and automobiles took over one piece of land after another. Today, the Wells Fargo company focuses on banking and no longer on express shipping.

Do you think that we should be sad about the end of the Pony Express? Well, it's understandable that when we see something as exciting as the Pony Express, we want it to last forever. However, it is essential to realize that even the founders of the company knew that it would only last for a little while. The important thing to realize is that all of those riders (there were eventually about 120 of them) worked hard to get a job done, and they earned the reputation as the bravest and most trustworthy mail carriers anywhere.

Even though the Pony Express only lasted about nineteen months, it played a hugely prominent role in American history and had lasting consequences as we will see in the next section.

Chapter 6: What Happened After the Pony Express?

After the Pony Express ended, everyone who had been involved went their separate ways. Some of them kept trying to make new businesses, others kept looking for adventure. For example, Buffalo Bill became one of the most famous Americans in the world for having a travelling show that talked all about the Wild West and including horse tricks, shooting, and reenactments of famous battles.

However, the Pony Express had affected at least one particularly significant part of American history: the role of California in the Civil War. Do you remember that we spoke earlier about how influential California was to both sides in the Civil War? California, because of the Gold Rush, had a large population and a lot of money. The 1860 census found that there were 379,985 people living in California, larger than the population of such eastern states as Vermont, New Hampshire, Delaware, and even Florida. That large number gave California increased voting power in the House of Representatives. As a result, both the North and the South wanted California on their side. However, when war finally broke out, California supplied troops and money to the Union, not to the Confederacy. What was a key factor in keeping California loyal to the Union? It was the Pony Express.

The Pony Express let the Federal Government keep good communication with California and to convince the people there to remain a part of the Union. With no communication coming from the South, the Californians felt no loyalty there. As a result, lots of California gold was sent to Union soldiers to buy weapons, food, and even things as simple as shoes. The Confederate army, without the sale of its profitable cotton and without outside help, soon entered into rough times, sometimes marching into battle with bare feet and empty stomachs.

California, because of the communication provided by the Pony Express and the Union loyalty that came with it, also helped to fight any possible rebellion within its borders and even over in New Mexico. The Union had gained a powerful and faithful friend when California joined its side. President Lincoln, the President of the Union during the Civil War, later wrote about how much he appreciated all that California had done. He said:

> "I have long desired to see California; the production of her gold mines has been a marvel to me, and her stand for the Union, her generous offerings to the Sanitary (Commission), and her loyal representatives have endeared your people to me; and nothing would give me more pleasure than a visit to the Pacific shore, and to say in person to your citizens, 'God bless you for your devotion to the Union,' but the unknown is before us. I may say, however, that I have it now in purpose when the railroad is finished, to visit your wonderful state."[5]

The Pony express, even though it lasted for such a short time, became an important part of the Old West, especially as we think about it today. Really, what symbol better sums up the tough conditions, the hard work ethic, and the danger that meant moving out west? Mark Twain, a famous American author, once wrote about the arrival of a Pony Express rider that he saw while travelling through the Old West. Have a look at how he describes the scene, in his book *Roughing It*:

> "In a little while all interest was taken up in stretching our necks and watching for the "pony-rider"—the fleet messenger who sped across the continent from St. Joe to Sacramento, carrying letters nineteen hundred miles in eight days! Think of that for perishable horse and human flesh

[5] Quotation source: http://www.parks.ca.gov/?page_id=26775

and blood to do! The pony-rider was usually a little bit of a man, brimful of spirit and endurance. No matter what time of the day or night his watch came on, and no matter whether it was winter or summer, raining, snowing, hailing, or sleeting, or whether his "beat" was a level straight road or a crazy trail over mountain crags and precipices, or whether it led through peaceful regions or regions that swarmed with hostile Indians, he must be always ready to leap into the saddle and be off like the wind! There was no idling-time for a pony-rider on duty. He rode fifty miles without stopping, by daylight, moonlight, starlight, or through the blackness of darkness—just as it happened. He rode a splendid horse that was born for a racer and fed and lodged like a gentleman; kept him at his utmost speed for ten miles, and then, as he came crashing up to the station where stood two men holding fast a fresh, impatient steed, the transfer of rider and mail-bag was made in the twinkling of an eye, and away flew the eager pair and were out of sight before the spectator could get hardly the ghost of a look. Both rider and horse went "flying light." The rider's dress was thin, and fitted close; he wore a "round-about," and a skull-cap, and tucked his pantaloons into his boot-tops like a race-rider. He carried no arms—he carried nothing that was not necessary, for even the postage on his literary freight was worth five dollars a letter. He got but little frivolous correspondence to carry—his bag had business letters in it, mostly. His horse was stripped of all unnecessary weight, too. He wore a little wafer of a racing-saddle, and no visible blanket. He wore light shoes, or none at all. The little flat mail-pockets strapped under the rider's thighs would each hold about the bulk of a child's primer. They held many and many an important business chapter and newspaper letter, but these were written on paper as airy and thin as gold-leaf, nearly, and thus bulk and weight were economized.

Every neck is stretched further, and every eye strained wider. Away across the endless dead level of the prairie a black speck appears against the sky, and it is plain that it moves. Well, I should think so!

In a second or two it becomes a horse and rider, rising and falling, rising and falling—sweeping toward us nearer and nearer—growing more and more distinct, more and more sharply defined—nearer and still nearer, and the flutter of the hoofs comes faintly to the ear—another instant a whoop and a hurrah from our upper deck, a wave of the rider's hand, but no reply, and man and horse burst past our excited faces, and go winging away like a belated fragment of a storm!

So sudden is it all, and so like a flash of unreal fancy, that but for the flake of white foam left quivering and perishing on a mail-sack after the vision had flashed by and disappeared, we might have doubted whether we had seen any actual horse and man at all, maybe."[6]

People loved the Pony Express, and down to this day when we think of the Wild West, we think of Cowboys, Native Americans, and the Pony Express.

---

[6] Quotation source: http://www.gutenberg.org/files/3177/3177-h/3177-h.htm#linkch08

Conclusion

We have learned a lot about the Pony Express. Let's have a brief review of the handbook.

First, we learned what led up to the Pony Express. For example, do you remember how so many people ended up living in California during the mid-1800s? It was because of the Gold Rush. Thousands and thousands of people moved to California to strike it rich, and many brought their families with them. All of these people, especially the businessmen and politicians wanted to send and receive letter from the East Coast. Do you remember what the other options for sending letters and small packages were? They could send packages by boat, but that could take up to a month. A stagecoach wasn't much better: it would take at least three or more weeks just to make it to Missouri.

Then, in the next section, we saw why the Pony Express was so necessary. As you will remember, communication was hugely important at that point in history because the Civil War was about to break out. Everyone wanted to California to be on their side, and people wanted to know what was happening on the other side of the country. Also, we saw how the Pony Express provided a service that no one else at the time could.

The section after that was exciting because we saw how the Pony Express was started and what some of the biggest challenges were. Remember, they had to build little stations along a 1,900 mile route and put about 400 horses along the way. Then, do you remember the kind of rider they were looking for? Like we learned, the Pony Express looked to hire young men who were orphans and paid them about $25 a week for their hard work. It was in that section that we saw the route that they travelled and see why these riders had to be fearless to do their job.

Then, the next section will gave us a chance to see what it was like to be a kid back then. We climbed into the saddle and rode along with the famous riders of the Pony Express (like Buffalo Bill) over mountains and across rivers to get the mail to its destination on time.

After that, we saw a little more about how the Pony Express ended. Even though it was a truly unique arrangement, the world changed mightily quickly and soon no one needed the Pony Express anymore. The two biggest changes were the telegraph and the railroad. The railroad could get people and letters from one coast of the country to the other even faster than the Pony Express could, and they never had to worry about tired horses.

Then, we found out what happened after. We saw how valuable California became in the Civil War, and how the legacy of the Pony Express rider lived on forever. Do you remember Mark Twain's exciting experience and how excited everyone was to see the Pony Express rider?

Even though we don't use telegraphs today, and most of us use cars, not trains, we should take some time to think about the Pony Express and the men who started it. Why should we care? The men who started and ran the Pony Express wanted to help people and to solve a problem that they saw. They used their own money, and they found people just as dedicated as they were to work hard and to get the job done. We have lots of problems today, and we need people who are willing to find good solutions and to take a risk to get the job done.

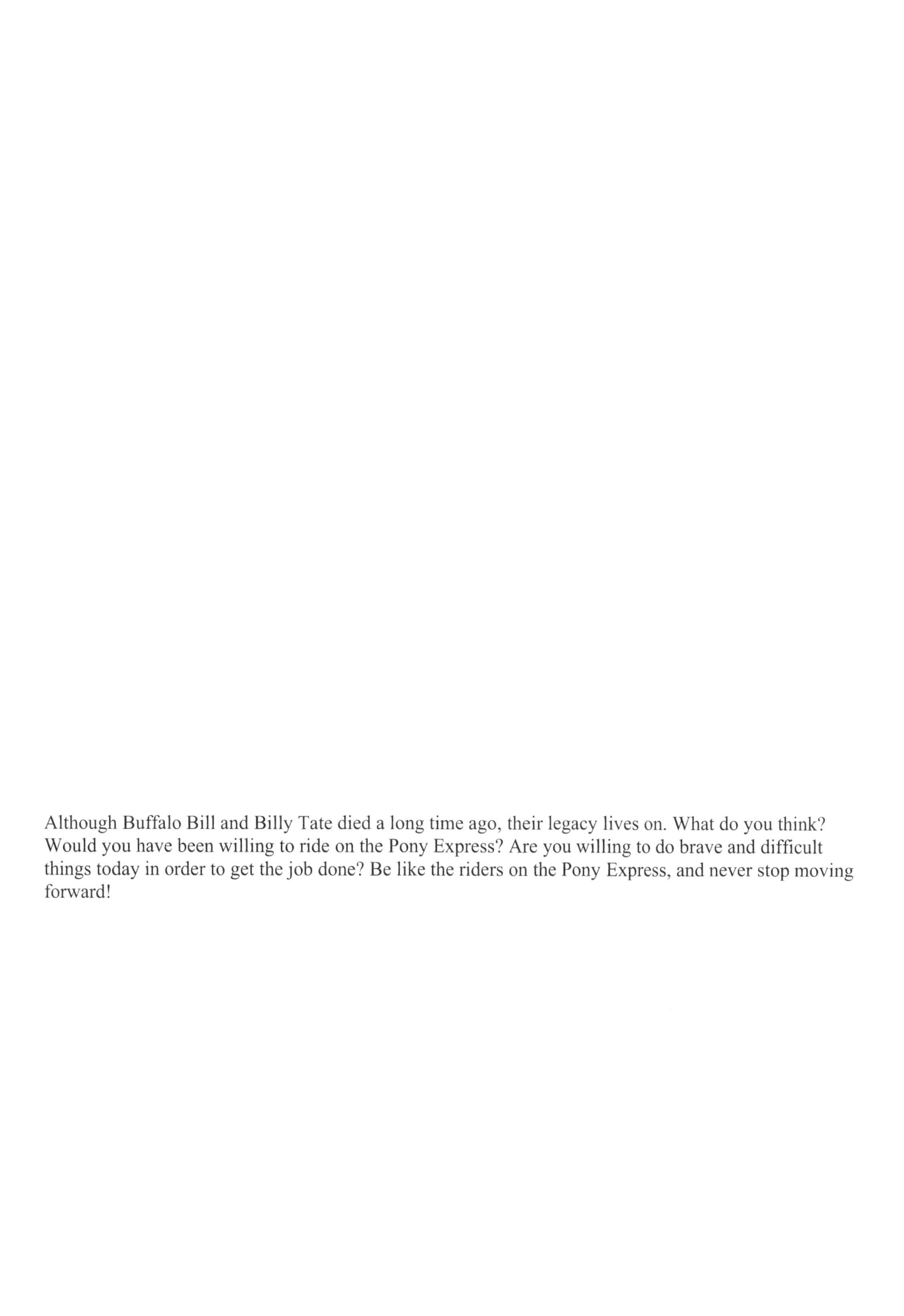

Although Buffalo Bill and Billy Tate died a long time ago, their legacy lives on. What do you think? Would you have been willing to ride on the Pony Express? Are you willing to do brave and difficult things today in order to get the job done? Be like the riders on the Pony Express, and never stop moving forward!

The Underground Railroad

Introduction

With each step, Joseph's feet bring him closer to freedom. He has been walking all night, and he is tired, but he dare not stop. He is sure that there are people looking for him; people who are walking with dogs, and with guns. He looks up to the night sky and sees that it is beautiful and full of stars. However, tonight, he is only focused on one star in particular. He remembers the song they taught him:

When the Sun comes back
And the first quail calls
Follow the Drinking Gourd,
For the old man is a-waiting for to carry you to freedom
If you follow the Drinking Gourd

The riverbank makes a very good road.
The dead trees will show you the way.
Left foot, peg foot, travelling on,
Follow the Drinking Gourd

Tonight, Joseph is following the Drinking Gourd. He knows that the Drinking Gourd is really code for the constellation of stars known as the Big Dipper. One star in this constellation, Polaris (also known as the North Star) will help Joseph to find his way to freedom. He is traveling from the Southern United States all the way up to the North, where friendly white people will help him.

Joseph is a slave. He is running away to freedom on the Underground Railroad.

Have you ever heard of the Underground Railroad before? What do you imagine in your mind? A lot of people think that there was an actual train, and that there were underground passages and tunnels. Well, when we are talking about the Underground Railroad, we aren't talking about either of those things. In reality, we are using the word "underground" to mean something that is hidden, and not seen by everyone. Also, the word "railroad" is used to describe the route that escaping slaves took when running away from the South to the North. In fact, there were lots of routes that people took to escape slavery.

So, when we talk about the Underground Railroad, we are talking about the places and people that secretly helped African American slaves get to freedom, especially during the years from 1850 to 1860, the time when thousands and thousands of runaway slaves used this Underground Railroad.

What do you think: was it easy to be a slave back then? Well, what do you know about slavery in the United States?

Slavery is when one person or group of people forces another person or group to work for them without paying them any money. This is what happened in the Unites States. White people made African Americans work for them without giving them any money. In fact, for many years on the United States, African Americans were treated like property; or even worse, they were treated like dumb animals. They were made to work long days in the hot sun, and weren't paid anything for it. They got some food and some old clothes every now and then, but they had to live in shacks with leaky roofs and dirt floors. Families were separated, and sometimes they never saw each other again. Can you imagine how they felt?

In the United States, slavery began early (in 1619) and lasted all the way until 1865, when it was outlawed by the Thirteenth Amendment. During these 246 years, about 600,000 African Americans were brought to the U.S. from Africa and mistreated and forced to do hard work. Many of them died from the mistreatment.

As more and more people began to disagree with the practice of slavery, the Underground Railroad came to life. What were the conditions that led to the formation of the Underground Railroad? What was it like to travel a slave from the enslaved South to the free North? What was it like to be a kid during those years, and when did people stop travelling on the Underground Railroad? We have a lot of interesting questions to answer, so let's get started.

Chapter 1: What led up to the Underground Railroad?

Before we understand what led to the Underground Railroad, we have to learn a little more about slavery itself. Slavery is a terrible thing-of that there can be no doubt. But how did slavery get started in the United States? Where did the slaves come from? How did they view their condition, and how did other people look at them?

The first slaves arrived in the United States in 1619, at the Jamestown colony (America's first permanent English settlement). They were brought there by Dutch traders. At the time, the Jamestown residents were still getting settled, so they needed all of the help that they could get. They welcomed the extra workers to help them build their homes, cultivate their fields, and protect themselves against the Native Americans. The African Americans who were sold to the Jamestown colonists were not treated as badly as others would be later on. In fact, most of them were treated like temporary workers, and were able to get their freedom later on and become landowners themselves.

As you may recall, the Jamestown colonists were originally sent from England to the New World as a sort of investment. The men who sent them, known as the London Company, wanted to start seeing a lot of money come in. This started to happen in 1612. John Rolfe, who would later become the husband of the famous Native American Pocahontas, was able to cultivate a sweet variety of tobacco in Virginia. Together, he and the other colonists began to cultivate larger and larger plantations of tobacco along the James River, sending more and more profits back to England.

For decades, the ones who did the actual work of digging in the fields, planting the seeds, and harvesting the leaves were indentured servants. Do you know what an indentured servant was? Well, an indentured servant was a person who wanted to get a fresh start in a new place and who was willing to work for it. In England, things were pretty tough, as far as work goes. The government didn't have a lot of money, and there weren't a lot of jobs available for young men to do. As a result, many of them decided that they wanted to go to the New World. After all, in a land of so much opportunity, there had to be a way for them to make some money!

But, how could a poor young man with no job afford the boat trip all the way across the Atlantic Ocean to the New World? Simply put: he couldn't. He had to find someone to help him. He had to become an indentured servant. An indentured servant is a poor person brought over from a faraway place to work. For example, they would come to the New World from England, and the plantation owners like John Rolfe would pay for their passage and give them a place to stay. In return they had to work for the owner for a number of years. Afterwards, they would be paid by the owner for their years of hard work and would be free to buy some land of their own. Not a bad arrangement, right?

This was the way that things were done for several decades in Jamestown and in the other colonies in the New World. However, things began to change in the 1660s and 1670s. Plantation owners, especially in Virginia and Maryland, began to prefer slave laborers, and not indentured servants. Why?

There were two main reasons: the first had to do with the economy in London, and the second had to do with the fears of the colonists.

> **Reason #1**: The economy in London had begun to steadily improve. Do you remember how plantation owners got so many people to work on their lands for them? They had indentured servants, men who came to the New World looking for work and exciting opportunities. But now that there was plenty of work in London and there was money to be made, fewer and fewer men came to the New World to work. What's more, the men who had come were finishing their contracts and were now looking for workers themselves. They needed to find a cheap source of labor and quickly.
>
> **Reason #2**: The colonists were afraid of having a lot of unemployed white men around. What were they afraid of? Well, do you remember something that happened in Jamestown in 1676, an event that came to be known as Bacon's Rebellion? Let's have a brief review. Nathaniel Bacon was a young white man who was not happy with how things were being done in the Virginia Government. He felt that the Governor should have been doing more to resolve the people's problems with Native Americans and to help them expand more into the frontier, into the West. He and a large group of white men eventually marched on the capital and burned it to the ground.
>
> The colonists living nearby were terrified. Many plantation owners saw these white men as a threat. They felt that the problem was that there was no work to keep them busy. After all, plantation owners weren't willing to pay them a decent wage in order to keep them employed. So the decision was made to rely less and less on indentured servants and white men, and more and more on African American slaves.

Gradually, colony after colony, from South Carolina all the way to New York, started to depend more and more on slave labor.

But where did all of the slaves come from? The slaves came from Africa, and they were sold to slave traders by fellow Africans. Can you imagine such a thing happening? How could that be? Well, remember that Africa is a large continent, and that it was inhabited by many different tribes and groups of people, many of them in conflict with one another. When there was a war, the winning side would often capture members of the opposing side's family, and sell them to slave traders. In other occasions, African slave traders would actually *kidnap* men, women, and even children to sell. It was terrible!

What would happen to these Africans after they were taken away from their families and villages? They were marched, often in chains, to places like the city of Ouidah, in what is now called Benin. This city was a place where future slaves were put into small huts and made to wait, sometimes for weeks or months, until the next trading ship passed by. When the ship arrived, often from England or from Portugal, it would be loaded up with Africans who would spend the next several weeks in the dark and damp hold of the ship. Some Africans would eat a mouthful of sand before they left, so that they would never forget their homeland. Can you imagine how sad they felt as they realized that they would never see their friends and family again?

What was it like once the Africans had boarded the ship, and what was it like during the trip? One man named Olaudah Equiano, who lived as a slave and then later was freed, described it like this:

> "The closeness of the place and the heat of the climate, added to the number in the ship, which was so crowded that each had scarcely room to turn himself, almost suffocated us. This produced copious perspirations, so that the air soon became unfit for respiration from a variety of loathsome smells, and brought on a sickness among the slaves, of which many died . . . The shrieks of the women and the groans of the dying rendered the whole a scene of horror almost inconceivable."

Can you imagine being treated like that? By the time that the ships arrived in the New World, an average of 20% of the slaves (or one out of every five) had died because of the terrible conditions.

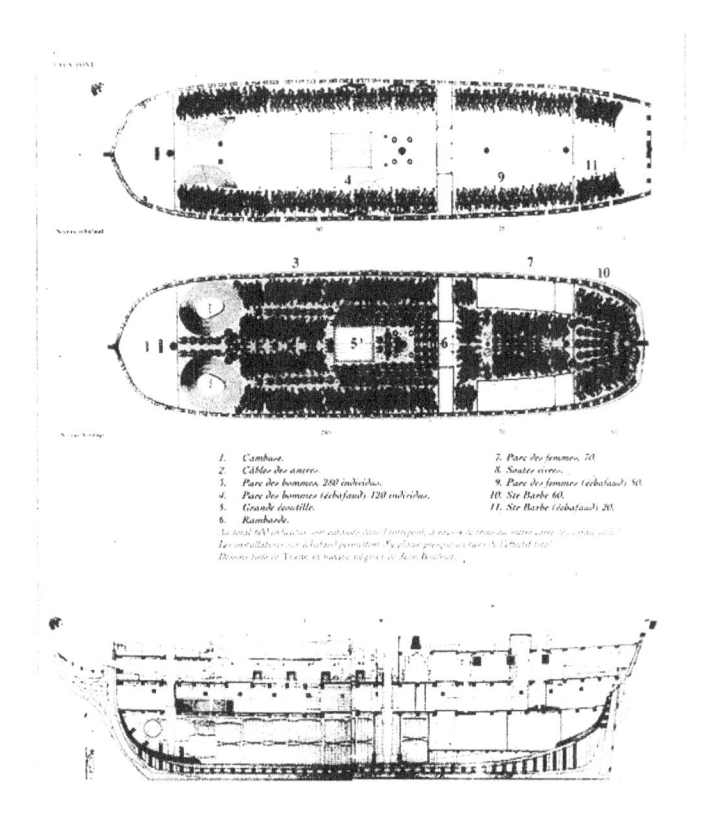

Once they _____ ere sold either individua_____ n you imagine how terrible it _____ see each other again? Can you i_____ ands and wives, brothers a_____ oodbye?

Their life of slavery had begun.

How did the slaves themselves view their situation? Their days would start early, going out into the fields while still dark. After the sun was up, they would come back and work closer to the house. They worked seven days a week with no days off. Their health was bad, the houses were small and shared by several families at the same time, and the work was hard.

As you can imagine, there was no way for them to be happy while being forced to work so hard for people who treated them so poorly. Many of them rebelled. In fact, these many rebellions actually forced the local state governments to make laws to regulate slavery.

For some time, the governments didn't really talk a whole lot about slavery. People practiced it, but the government didn't really get too involved. However, as the slaves themselves began to have babies, there was a question: are the babies born to slave mothers free people or should they be treated like their slave mothers? If a white owner has a baby with his slave, should he be forced to take care of it? In 1662, the government of Virginia, known as the House of Burgesses, passed a law saying that the child shall be born into the same condition as the mother. If the mother is free, the child shall be free. If the mother is a slave, then that child would be one also.

This was a sneaky thing to do. For years, the colonists had been under the English way of doing things (that the child will be like his father) but as many white slave owners began to abuse and even rape their slave women, many pregnancies resulted. These awful men wanted to hide what they had done and not have to view the child as their own. Can you believe that! These men didn't want to take care of their own children! They wanted to pretend that the child belonged to another man and that nothing had ever happened between him and the girl! What do you think about that?

In 1691, Virginia approved a series of laws known as "slave codes" that detailed how slaves should be treated. It said that they could not be freed by their owners, only under very specific conditions and for a high cost (people thought that having a lot of free African Americans walking around would lead to lots of slave rebellions). They also stated that a slave could not marry a white person, could not vote, could not hold public office, and could not use a weapon. In 1696, South Carolina passed its own slave code, which officially said that slaves were officially property of their owners and that they had no right to life (which meant that the owner could kill a slave and no one would ask any questions, not even the police!).

Throughout the years, more and more slaves began to resent the life that they had been forced into. In one place after another, there were "revolts" or rebellions, against slave owners and white people in general. In fact, some of these rebellions even had the support, help, and participation of a few brave white people. Let's have a look at some of them.

1712, New York City: This was the first sizeable slave revolt in the New World. In New York City, there were a number of free African Americans and a huge number of African American slaves. However, the two groups could easily meet together and make plans. They decided to get their revenge on some of the white people who were making their lives so terrible.

On the night of April 6, a group of 23 African American men set fire to a building. When white colonists came to put it out, the men (who had been hiding nearby) attacked them. They killed nine white colonists and injured six more.

The government was swift in its response. Over 70 African Americans were arrested, and 21 of them were convicted and executed (twenty were burned to death and one was tortured to death on a breaking wheel).

After the rebellion, New York put some strong laws in place in order to limit the freedoms of slaves even more. African Americans were not allowed to meet in groups of more than three; they could not carry guns at any time; and any owner who wanted to free his slaves had to pay a very high price (higher than the cost of buying a new slave).

1739, South Carolina: On the night of September 9, a slave named Jemmy, belonging to the Cato family, gathered a group of about twenty slaves and began to march South, toward Spanish Florida (a safe place for escaped slaves). With a large banner reading "liberty" the men marched down the Stono River. They attacked a shop, killed two white men and got some weapons and ammunition. Continuing their march, the eventually recruited about 60 more slaves, burned seven plantations to the ground, and killed more than twenty white men along the way.

The next day, a militia made up of plantation owners and slaveholders fought with the group, killing most of them (the rest would be killed or captured within a week). The heads of the rebel slaves were cut off and put on posts along major roads in order to warn other slaves of the consequences of rebellion. That's pretty gross, right? What would you have thought if you saw a bunch of heads on the side of the road like that?

As a direct result of this rebellion (the most successful up to that time) South Carolina passed the Negro Act of 1740. This act included some important laws. It prevented slaves from gathering together, from learning to read English, and from earning money for themselves. It also officially gave owners the right to kill rebellious slaves (although they had been doing that anyway).

1800, Virginia: Gabriel Prosser, a slave who worked as a blacksmith, planned a large uprising of several hundred slaves for the night of August 30, 1800. Two of his fellow slaves turned him in, and he was captured and hung along with twenty five other slaves. Although they were not successful, this planned rebellion made a lot of people afraid, mainly because there were so many slaves and so few white males in the area.

What's more, other nations (like France) had made slavery illegal. The largest slave rebellion in history, in modern day Haiti, was happening at the same time, and would eventually lead to the freedom of thousands of slaves. News of the successful Haitian rebellion made American slaves hopeful. They thought that maybe, just maybe, they could rebel against their masters and fight for their freedom.

1831, Virginia: Nat Turner began a revolution with about 70 slaves on August 21, and the rebellion lasted for 48 hours. They entered into homes of slave owners and killed all of the white people that they could find, and freed the slaves that they found. Local militia and government troops got involved quickly and brought the rebellion to an end.

Although it was very short, the rebellion had terrible repercussions. Many of the white people living in the area were convinced that it had been part of a larger, countrywide rebellion. There were wild stories of groups of armed slaves marching in every city, killing all of the white people that they saw. As a result, local militias made up of scared colonists showed little control and began to violently attack and kill many slaves whom they suspected had been involved, although there was no proof against them and there had been no legal trial. It is estimated that over 200 slaves died as a result of militia activity, far more than were actually involved in the rebellion. This means that many innocent slaves were killed, just for being in the wrong place at the wrong time.

1859, Virginia: An abolitionist (a white person who fights against slavery) named John Brown attacked a military weapons storage facility in Harpers Ferry on the night of October 16. He was convinced that he could break into the storage facility, steal the weapons, and arm the local slaves. With their help, he could travel from town to town, arming the slaves and forcing the Virginia slaveholders into a panic. It would be the beginning of the fight for freedom for Virginia slaves…or so he thought.

The raid did not go as he had planned. Although John Brown had hoped to have over 200 slaves fighting alongside him that first night, none actually joined him. Within three days, every member of his group of 21 men was either dead or arrested, and John Brown himself had been killed with a sword.

As you can see, slavery was a terrible institution, and those who revolted against it usually met with death and violence. There had to be another way for people to escape from slavery.

Chapter 2: Why did the Underground Railroad happen?

As we have already discussed, slavery was a terrible thing. African Americans were treated like property, and sometimes even like animals. Even so, slavery was tolerated in the United States for over 200 years. What finally led to the formation of the Underground Railroad, especially in the years from 1850 to 1860?

The main reason had to do with the different cultures in the Northern United States and in the Southern United States. After the American Revolution had been successfully concluded in 1783, all of the Northern states banned slavery officially (the final state to do so was New Jersey, in 1804). As a result, states like New York, Connecticut and Pennsylvania were safe places to be an African American. There, African Americans they could marry, own land, do business, and raise families- all without fear of being mistreated or enslaved.

Southern states, on the other hand still relied heavily on slave labor to keep their economy strong. They grew crops that were very labor intensive (that means that it took a lot of work to grow these crops). Especially in the first half of the 1800s, when cotton began to be cultivated as a cash crop (a crop that makes a lot of money) Southerners depended more than ever on large numbers of slaves working in the fields.

For some time, many Northerners didn't like slavery, but they didn't have to support it themselves. It reality, they didn't even have to think about it too much. The problem was bad, but, after all, it was happening very far away.

All of that changed in 1850.

The United States government had been struggling for some time with what to do with its new territories. Places like Texas, New Mexico, Kansas, and California had all become part of the United States, but there weren't strict laws yet about how life would be there. For example, would the new territories be allowed to have slaves? The South wanted slaves to be allowed, but the North didn't.

As the arguments in Washington D.C. got more and more intense, it looked like a war was going to break out between the two sides. Finally, a series of five decisions were approved in 1850, and together they were called "The Compromise of 1850". These laws were meant to keep peace between the two sides, both of which felt strongly about slavery. One of the laws passed was called the Fugitive Slave Act of 1850. What did this law say?

Well, as we learned, the North was a much safer place to be African American than in the South. As a result, many slaves would try to escape their masters and head north. The Northerners would welcome them and help them to get established. If the master came looking for the runaway slave, the Northerners were not obligated to help him, and the slave could stay free. It was a way for the Northerners to oppose the slavery that they hated so much.

The Fugitive Slave Act of 18[...]rn States to help the Southern slaveholders. It made them h[...] would put sheriffs and private citizens in jail if they didn't [...]

What do you think about that? Do you think that the Northerners appreciated being forced to support slavery? In other words, they had to help slave owners stay in business, and keep doing cruel things to their slaves? What would you have done if you found a runaway slave in the North? Would you have helped him or would you have turned him in?

The Fugitive Slave Act of 1850 forced the Northerners to stand up for what they believed in. Religious people in the North (especially members of the Quaker Church) felt that it was just wrong to treat fellow humans the way that slaves were being treated. Freed African Americans and whites got together, and decided to find a way to help escaped slaves get to Canada. Why Canada? Well, any escaped slave found in Northern states could still be hunted down and returned. But Canada had no laws like the Fugitive Slave Act of 1850, and would protect any slaves that made it that far north.

As a direct result of a law meant to stop slaves from running away, the Underground Railroad became stronger and better established than ever, and helped thousands of slaves to find their freedom.

Chapter 3: What Happened on the Underground Railroad?

There was not just one route used during the era of the Underground Railroad. In fact, there were dozens of them stretching across the country. There were hundreds of people involved who helped thousands of slaves to escape. Altogether, they formed the "Underground Railroad".

The first traces of an organized system to help slaves escape was actually back in 1693, when the Spanish (who were in control of Florida at the time) offered all escaped slaves asylum. The term "asylum" meant that they would give the slaves freedom and that they would protect them from anyone who wanted to hurt them; the Spanish would do this for the slaves only if they promised to be loyal both to the Spanish government and to the Catholic Church. For some time, all African American escape attempts focused on going south.

However, by 1834, Florida was no longer under Spanish control, and Canada (as a British colony) had officially outlawed slavery; so the Far North became the new destination for runaway slaves.

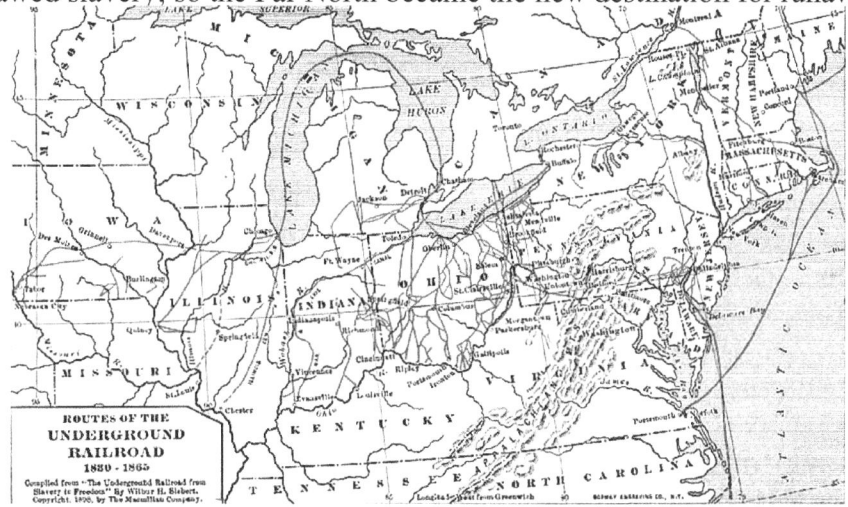

If they were, he would make arrangements for small groups, sometimes of just one to three slaves, to escape along a special route. These routes would take them from one place to another, all the way to Canada. They would travel at night to avoid being seen, and rest at different stops along the way. Using this method, between 30,000 and 100,000 slaves escaped to Canada by the time the U.S. Civil war broke out.

At this time in history, the steam engine train was becoming more and more important. It was used to move goods and people all across the country, and even into new territories. Because of its popularity, those people who were helping the slaves to escape decided to use some vocabulary worked related to trains to describe their work. This served to hide what they were doing from anyone who happened to find their notes or overhear them speaking. Historian David Blight includes the following terms in his book *Passages to Freedom: The Underground Railroad in History and Memory*:

- People who helped slaves find the railroad were **agents**
- Guides were known as **conductors**
- Free or escaped blacks (or sometimes whites) who helped guide fugitives were **abductors**
- Hiding places were **stations**

- **Station masters** hid slaves in their homes
- Escaped slaves were referred to as **passengers** or **cargo**

There were a lot of very important people who helped to make the Underground Railroad a success. Think of the farmers and their families who had to put food and bedding in secret places for the runaway slaves. What would have happened if they told someone what they were doing? Under the Fugitive Slave Act of 1850, the slave would have been caught and returned to his owner, and the whole family would have gone to jail. Would you have been too afraid to help, or would you have let runaway slaves rest at your house during the day?

Although a lot of people worked together to bring the African American slaves freedom, a few really stand out for their efforts. One of them was William Still. William Still was born free, the son of a slave, in Philadelphia, Pennsylvania. By the time he reached his 30s, he had become a leader of the African American community in Philadelphia, and was working hard to abolish slavery. Because of his amazing efforts and ability to organize, he is known today as "the father of the Underground Railroad". He helped as many as 60 slaves each month to escape, and he kept detailed records with names and personal information. He even became a courier of sorts, carrying messages back and forth from escaped slaves and their families who had to stay behind.

Another very important person on the Underground Railroad was Harriet Tubman. Born a slave, she herself escaped from Maryland into free Philadelphia. Once there, she felt a special obligation to return to Maryland and to help her family escape. Over the next thirteen years, she made eleven trips back to Maryland, eventually helping a total of 70 family members and friends to escape, she herself personally guiding them along the way. She never lost a "passenger". After the Fugitive Slave Act of 1850, she began guiding escaped slaves into Canada.

What do you think it was like back then to help an escaped slave? Do you think that it was easy for men and women like William Still and Harriet Tubman to risk their lives, time after time after time? Do you think they did the right thing by ignoring the Fugitive Slave Act?

Other than the special vocabulary and the assistance they received along the way, what else helped the escaping slaves to avoid getting lost while traveling the Underground Railroad, and to make their way to freedom? Do you remember song that we saw in the introduction? It went like this:

When the Sun comes back
And the first quail calls
Follow the Drinking Gourd,
For the old man is a-waiting for to carry you to freedom
If you follow the Drinking Gourd

The riverbank makes a very good road.
The dead trees will show you the way.
Left foot, peg foot, travelling on,
Follow the Drinking Gourd

This song was also full of code and hints to help the runaway slaves. As we saw, the "Drinking Gourd" referred to the Big Dipper, which helped the slaves to identify the North Star, and thus which direction to move in. What other codes did it have?

"**When the Sun comes back and the first quail calls**" both talk about the arrival of spring in the South. It was the best time to travel, when there was still ice on the rivers (making them easier to cross) but it was not too cold to be moving around at night.

"**For the old man is a-waiting for to carry you to freedom**" talks about a famous guide who would meet the slaves on a certain trail each spring. His name was Peg Leg Joe (his right leg was missing, and he had a wooden stick there instead).

"**The riverbank makes a very good road. The dead trees will show you the way**." This describes the route along the Ohio River that many slaves took, and how they could avoid detection and getting lost by staying close to the river.

"**Left foot, peg foot, travelling on.**" This line talks about the strange prints left by the one legged Peg Leg Joe. By staying close to him, the slaves would find their way to the next safe house, and then on to freedom.

This song (and others like it) was important to the runaway slaves. It gave them directions and a sense of hope. It let them know that they were not alone, and that they would find people along the way to make their journey easier.

For the thousands of slaves who made the journey on the Underground Railroad, their freedom was just around the corner.

Chapter 4: What was it like to be a Kid During the Time of the Underground Railroad?

As we have spoken about a little bit, it would have been a very challenging time to be a kid back then. Let's look at it from two sides: being a free white kid, and being a kid who was born an African American slave.

A free white kid: If you were born a free white kid back then, you would have seen a lot of terrible things happen to African American slaves. You would have seen slaves get beaten for making a small mistake, like letting soup get too hot. You would have seen African American men get hung for crimes that they did not commit, and you would have seen whole families ripped apart at slave auctions. If your family owned slaves, how would you have felt about it? Would you have supported the slaves and tried to treat them nicer than other people did? Would you have treated the slaves badly and been angry at people who tried to stop you?

As you heard your parents talking about the way that the different states felt about slavery, would you have been afraid of a coming Civil War?

If you lived in the North, and you saw a fugitive slave hiding at a neighbor's house, do you think that you would have called the police? After all, that's what the law said you had to do. Why do you think that white people tolerated slavery for so long? Is it because they were all bad? Not really. A lot of white slave owners were just doing what their parents had done. In fact, the government and even some church leaders said that slavery was okay, so they didn't think that they were doing anything wrong.

A kid who was born an African American slave: Now, think about what it would have been like to have been born a slave. Every time you woke up, you would have to think about what other people wanted you to do. You would have to work hard and not get paid. You would see your family members get beaten or even killed by the master. You would not have the freedom to become what you want to be; you could only become what the master allowed.

Under many of the slave laws passed in the Southern United States, African Americans weren't even allowed to read. Think about that for a moment. What would your life be like if you couldn't read? Well, you wouldn't be learning about the Underground Railroad from this handout, would you? You couldn't go to school to become a doctor or a lawyer, you couldn't write songs, and you couldn't write letters to your family. What's more, if you wanted to do something other than be a slave, tough luck! You would have no choice. You would have to work where the master told you, how the master told you, when the master told you. If you made a mistake, the punishment would be severe.

Being a kid in those days, whether you were white or African American, wasn't an easy thing to do. You would have had to decide how you felt about slavery, and then do something about it. If you were white, you could try to help the slaves to run away. If you African American, you could try to run away yourself, and then help others to do the same.

Chapter 5: How did the Underground Railroad Come to an End?

The Underground Railroad was very important when slavery was still legal in parts of the United States. However, once slavery became illegal (against the law) there was no longer a need for the Underground

Railroad. So, when and how did slavery become illegal in the United States? Well, it was a gradual process, but there were several important moments along the way. Let's look at a few of them.

- **The United States Civil War breaks out**
- **The Emancipation Proclamation**
- **The Thirteenth Amendment**

The United States Civil War breaks out. As we saw earlier, the Southern states had been pushing more and more for the new U.S. territories to allow slavery. On the other hand, the recently elected President in 1861, Abraham Lincoln, had promised during his campaign that he would never allow such a thing to happen. Shortly before he took office, seven slave states rebelled against the U.S. Federal government and formed their own government, called the Confederate States of America. On April 12, 1861, armies from this new nation attacked Fort Sumter in South Carolina. Lincoln called for troops from each state to go and fight against the rebels, which caused four more slave states to join the Confederates.

The American Civil War had begun. This war, which had the issue of slavery at its center, would determine the fate of thousands and thousands of African American slaves across the country. It was about this time that the Underground Railroad stopped transporting slaves to Canada. In fact, many slaves who had fled to Canada came back to fight alongside Union (Federal) soldiers in the conflict. They knew that, if the Union won, they would be able to see their fellow African Americans set free.

The Emancipation Proclamation. The President of the United States has special authority given to him during a time of war. When the Civil War broke out, President Lincoln used this authority to make a very special law that only applied to the states that were still rebelling in January of 1863. Earlier, after the Confederates had lost a large battle in a place called Antietam, Lincoln told them in September of 1862 that they had until January of the following year before he would issue this special proclamation with his powers as president. When the states did not respond, the Emancipation Proclamation went into effect on January 1, 1863. All African American slaves living within the borders of the rebel states were officially freed from their slavery. How do you think those slaves felt when they heard the news? Do you think they celebrated? Were there any parties that night? Or were they afraid of what their masters would do?

As the Union army marched into each town and state, they would free all of the slaves that they found. Many of the freed African American men would choose to join the army and fight to free other slaves.

The Thirteenth Amendment. After the American Civil War had ended, the Federal government was worried that some people would think that the freeing of the slaves had been something temporary, only meant to last as long as there was a war raging on. In order to make sure that everyone knew that slavery was never again to be allowed in the United States, the Thirteenth Amendment was adopted in December of 1865. It says, in part:

> "Neither slavery nor involuntary servitude, except as a punishment for crime whereof the party shall have been duly convicted, shall exist within the United States, or any place subject to their jurisdiction."

Do you understand how important those words were to the thousands of men, women, and children who had lived as slaves? These words guaranteed that no one, no matter how much money they had or where they lived, could force them to become slaves again. They were *free*, they were *finally free*!

Chapter 6: What Happened After the Underground Railroad?

After the Civil War ended, all slaves were freed. There was no Underground Railroad anymore because there were no more slaves to free. But did that mean the troubles were over for African Americans living in the United States? When were African Americans finally viewed as equal to white people? What happened to the South after all of the slaves went free? Let's find out.

African Americans who were freed no longer had to live as slaves, and that was a great thing. However, they still had a lot of hurdles to overcome. For example, most former slaves did not know how to read or write and had not been allowed to attend public school. As a result, they had trouble finding work. The war had hurt the South economically, and so landowners had little money to pay workers. Things were tough.

What's more, even though they were no longer slaves, many African Americans were still treated very poorly by whites. Sometimes, they were treated like unintelligent people and second rate citizens. In fact, in 1891, the Supreme Court of the United States said that individual states (especially those in the South) could separate African Americans and whites in everyday life. They used the phrase "separate but equal" to describe the system.

This idea of separating whites and African Americans lasted all the way until the civil rights movements of the 1960s. In fact, for a long time, it was illegal for African Americans to vote and share buses and train cars with, and even to marry white people. Here is a brief list of the victories won by African Americans in their efforts to be seen as equal citizens:

- **December 1865**: Thirteenth Amendment is adopted
- **February 1870**: African American males allowed to vote
- **July 1948**: The U.S. military is desegregated
- **May 1954**: No more segregation in schools
- **November 1956**: Desegregation of public transport in Alabama
- **January 1990**: First African American elected governor
- **January 1993**: First African American female elected to U.S. Senate
- **January 2009**: First African American elected to the office of the U.S. Presidency

Of course, there were other important moments, but these were some of the most exciting ones as they show how African Americans were gradually earning equality in the United States.

What happened to the South after all of the African American slaves either escaped through the Underground Railroad or who were freed by the government? The economy really slowed down, and it took a while for things to recover. Farms had been destroyed, tools were nowhere to be seen, and machinery, necessary to replace the backbreaking labor done by the slaves, had to be purchased. Over 25% of the Southern workforce had died in the war, so things were difficult.

The Southerners had to start their lives all over again.

Conclusion

Today, we no longer see slavery in the United States. We don't see slave masters whipping men, women, and children, and we can be very grateful for that. We don't see people sweating in the hot sun while others yell at them to work faster, harder, and better. We don't see violent rebellions or terrible civil wars. We don't see the Underground Railroad in operation anymore- it had served its purpose, so it went away.

Slavery was a very sad part of American history. It was a time people were judged according to the value of their skin. There were valued only as far as how they looked. If they had the wrong skin color, they couldn't vote, defend themselves to the police, or even get married to the person that they loved. Aren't you glad that slavery doesn't exist anymore?

One of the biggest helps to slaves was the Underground Railroad. This was a system where people, both African American and white, helped slaves escape to the free North. Do you remember the song that they sang along the way to help them? Do you remember the code words used by the people along the way?

It took a lot of courage to do what was right back then. After all, the laws actually protected the slaveholders, and not the slaves themselves. If you had tried to help a runaway slave, you could've gotten into trouble also.

After the Civil War, slaves were freed, but it still took some time until everyone could see them as equals, as human beings worthy of respect and friendship. If you had lived in the time when people treated African American's differently, would you have had the courage to be different?

Today, none of us are slaves, and we are really happy about that. Because of the fights that the African Americans fought, there are now laws in place that protect all of us, no matter what color we are. But, do you think that we have earned an important lesson from all of this? We have seen the dangers of showing prejudice. What is prejudice? Well, it is when we judge someone, or make an opinion about the,, before we even know them. We might do it because of the color of their skin, their religion, the way they look or talk, or even the way they dress. Do you think it is right to do that?

History has shown us that, when we treat people poorly just because they are different, we hurt everybody, including ourselves. Think of all of the suffering that resulted from the slave rebellions and the Civil War- all of the suffering could have been avoided.

The Underground Railroad was a chance for people to stand up against something that they knew was wrong. It let them help those who were victims, and be a part of the solution instead of the problem. What do you think? The next time that you see someone who is being mistreated, will you have the courage to stand up and help them? If you do, you will be just like the people who were brave enough to work and travel on the Underground Railroad!

The California Gold Rush

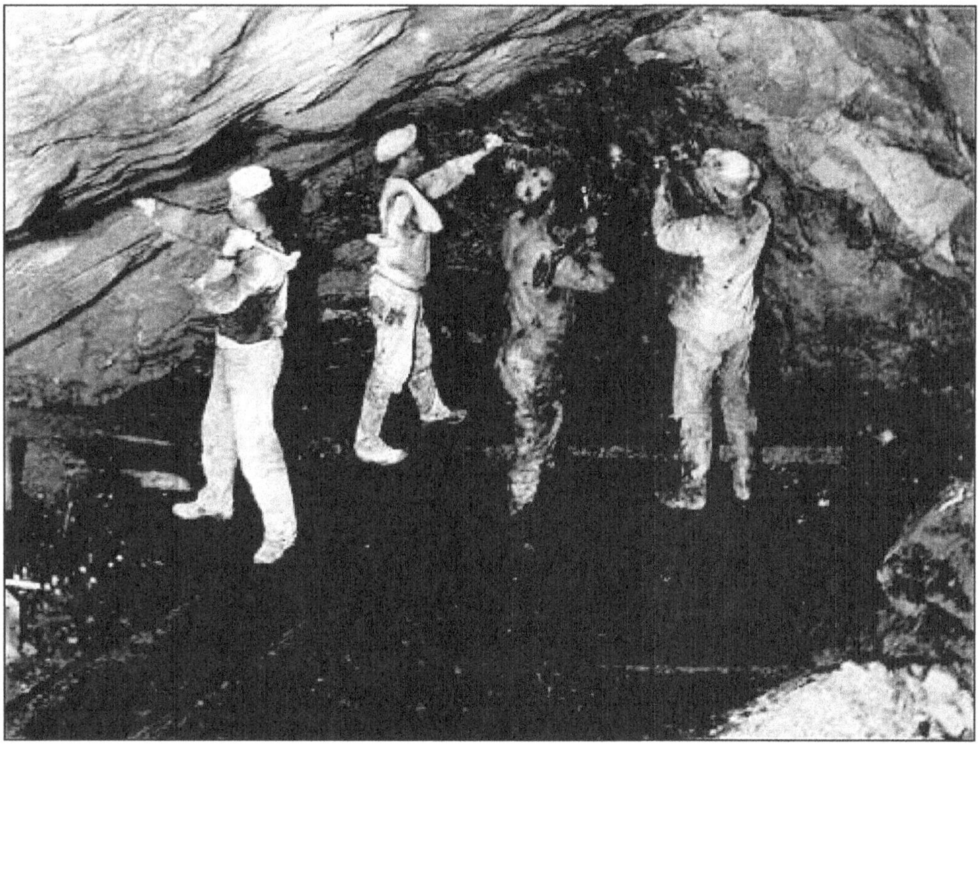

Introduction

The long car carried the men down into the depths of the Empire Gold Mine outside of Grass Valley, California. The year is 1850. These men are working to find and extract gold from the hard quartz rock in the Foothill Mountains of California. The tunnel that they were descending down wasn't very high, so they had to watch their heads. There they were, a line of men, one seated behind the other, moving slowly down a track.

One half mile (about 2500 feet) above them, their coworkers worked with a large motor that released the tension on a length of rope and thus lowered them further and further down into the black depths below. They still had another 2500 feet to travel before they reached the bottom.

Once they get to the bottom, the men are able to stand up completely. It is like another world down here in the mine, 5,000 feet (nearly one mile) below the surface. The mining here goes on twenty four hours a day. Even as they are arriving, another group of men is climbing into the car that they just got out of. A moment later, they see the little car behind them taken back up. In a few minutes, it will come back down with more workers, and the process will be repeated. The miners will be here for the next 10 hours, until their shift has ended. They turn on the lights on their hardhats and walk further into the mine.

Large pipes go past them. The pipes are connected to large steam engines on the surface. Running twenty four hours a day, these engines continuously pump out the water from the deepest parts of the mine shafts. If these pumps stopped working for even a few hours, the miners would most likely drown in the water that would quickly rise up. It can be scary down here, but it is no place to panic. A man has to keep a cool head about him. There are over 2.5 miles of tunnel down here, and it is easy to get lost. The workers stayed together and followed the noise of the others working and shouting ahead of them.

After a short walk, they saw their coworkers. Using large hammers and chisels, the men were putting deep, round holes into the tough rock on the walls of the tunnel. After they had made several holes, a different worker came and carefully placed a stick of dynamite in each hole. He placed a blasting cap on the end of each stick, which was already connected to the wires leading back to the detonating handle. The warning was given, and all of the men moved a safe distance away from the scene. As soon as everyone was accounted for, the blasting caps were detonated, causing a huge explosion. Up on the surface, explosions like this one would be heard far away from the mine, 24 hours a day, six days a week.

Once the smoke had cleared and all of the dust had settled, the miners would go back to the work area and begin to put the rocks into heavy metal carts. The carts, once full, would be pulled out of the way by donkeys that lived underground, seven carts at a time. Then, they would be pulled the 5,000 foot distance all the way to the surface. While the men below kept blasting the rock loose and digging the tunnel deeper and deeper, a few inches at a time, the men above would get to work crushing the chunks of quartz (called "ore") that had come up in the carts. They would pound the rocks into a fine dust using a stamp mill, which was a series of heavy mechanical hammers. Then, using a special chemical process, they would separate the gold flakes from the rock dust. For every two thousand pounds of rocks that they smashed and cleaned, they would get about one ounce of gold. Even that small amount of gold was enough to make them a nice profit.

Yes, it was the height of the gold rush in California, USA. What do you know about the 1849 gold rush? It was a very exciting time in the United States. People were looking everywhere for gold: in streams, underground, and in the mountains. They were even diverting entire rivers in order to get access to the dry riverbed below, to see if there was any gold there! It was a time when everybody who heard about it started thinking about striking it rich and becoming wealthy overnight.

The 1849 gold rush had small beginnings, as we will see. However, soon after it started, hundreds of thousands of people would come from all over the world to try their hand at gold prospecting and see what they could find. Friendships and alliances would be formed, and enemies would be made. Before the gold rush peaked in 1852, over $2 billion in gold will have been panned, mined, and sold. Some people will have died trying to get rich; others will have died trying to stop all of the new arrivals to California from destroying the area looking for gold. Entire ethnic groups will have become the targets of terrible treatment and outright persecution, while others will have become richer than their wildest dreams. The gold rush was a very unique time in American history.

In this report, we will be taking a closer look at this momentous period. We will find out why there was so much gold in California in the first place, and how it came to be discovered by and belong to Americans. We will have a look at why so many people came running to California, and what some of the immediate and long term consequences were. We will hear tales of success and of heartbreaking tragedy. We will learn what it was like to be a kid in those days, and about how the gold rush finally ended.

This handbook is also going to teach us some very important key terms that will help us to understand this period better. For example, we will learn about a philosophy called Manifest Destiny, about the different methods used to get gold out of the earth (like Placer mining and hard Rock mining) and about the real impact of the gold rush on history. You might be surprised when we discuss how important the gold rush really was to American history. It's safe to say that, if it weren't for the gold rush, America today would be very different.

Are you ready to start learning more? Then let's begin!

Chapter 1: What led up to the Gold Rush?

You might ask yourself: why was there so much gold in California? That's a great question. To find out the answer, we have to go back in time about 400 million years. Do you know where California was found 400 million years ago? It was at the bottom of the ocean. The land that we know as California hadn't yet been pushed up out of the water by tectonic plate movement. What was going on while the land was underwater? For thousands of years, volcanic activity went pushing out lots and lots of liquid magma (molten lava) all over the surface of the ocean floor (which would later rise to the surface and become California). The magma carried with it lots of minerals- including gold- which then covered the surface of the ground. Eventually, these minerals cooled off, hardened, and formed streams inside the solidified quartz rocks.

As time went by, the constant movement of the tectonic plates forced the land that would become California up to the surface, carrying the streams of gold in the quartz rocks with it. Primarily found in the Sierra Nevada mountain range, the gold was slowly eroded away by thousands of years of wind and rainstorms. It flowed down the mountainsides into streams and rivers, which later got smaller and smaller or dried up entirely. The gold, sometimes in chunks called "nuggets", other times in flakes or dust, would stay in the loose gravel on the sides of the streams. There it lay for thousands and thousands of years, until the prospectors of the Gold Rush found it.

It is amazing to think that such huge quantities of gold were just sitting there, so easily accessible, for such a long period of time. Why didn't the Native American population who had been living in California start gathering it? Well, simply put, Native Americans didn't value gold as much as other cultures (like Europeans). For them, feathers, animal furs, and shells were much more valuable and useful than small yellow pieces of soft rock. It wasn't until American settlers arrived in the mid-1800s that anyone started to notice to all of the gold literally just lying around. But how did it come to be that American settlers were in California in the first place to find all that gold?

California, previously called "Alta California", used to belong to Spain, and then to independent Mexico. It was first explored in depth by Spanish missionaries who moved steadily northward from Mexico, establishing missions and spreading their religion to the native peoples. Once they became independent, Mexico came to own a large part of what is now the United States. Their territory included California, Nevada, Utah, and Arizona. However, all of that changed with the Mexican-American War that broke out in 1846.

In 1836, the Republic of Texas had declared their independence from Mexico. During the years that followed, there was constant fighting about where exactly the border between the new Republic of Texas and the country of Mexico was. What's more, as Texas began to be considered for statehood in the United States (something that would eventually happen on December 19, 1845) Mexico began to threaten the United States. Their officials said that if the United States accepted Texas as a state there would be a war. How would the Americans react?

For reasons that we will see in the next section, the President at the time, James Polk, was very interested in pushing westward. For him, Texas was worth fighting for. During the two year war that followed (called the Mexican-American War) Mexico's soldiers lost battle after battle, most of which were fought on Mexican soil. Finally, on 2 February 1848, the Treaty of Guadalupe Hidalgo was signed in Mexico City, officially ending the Mexican-American War. In addition to ending the fighting, the treaty also included some very interesting details as far as the territory including California was involved: the land would be ceded to the United States.

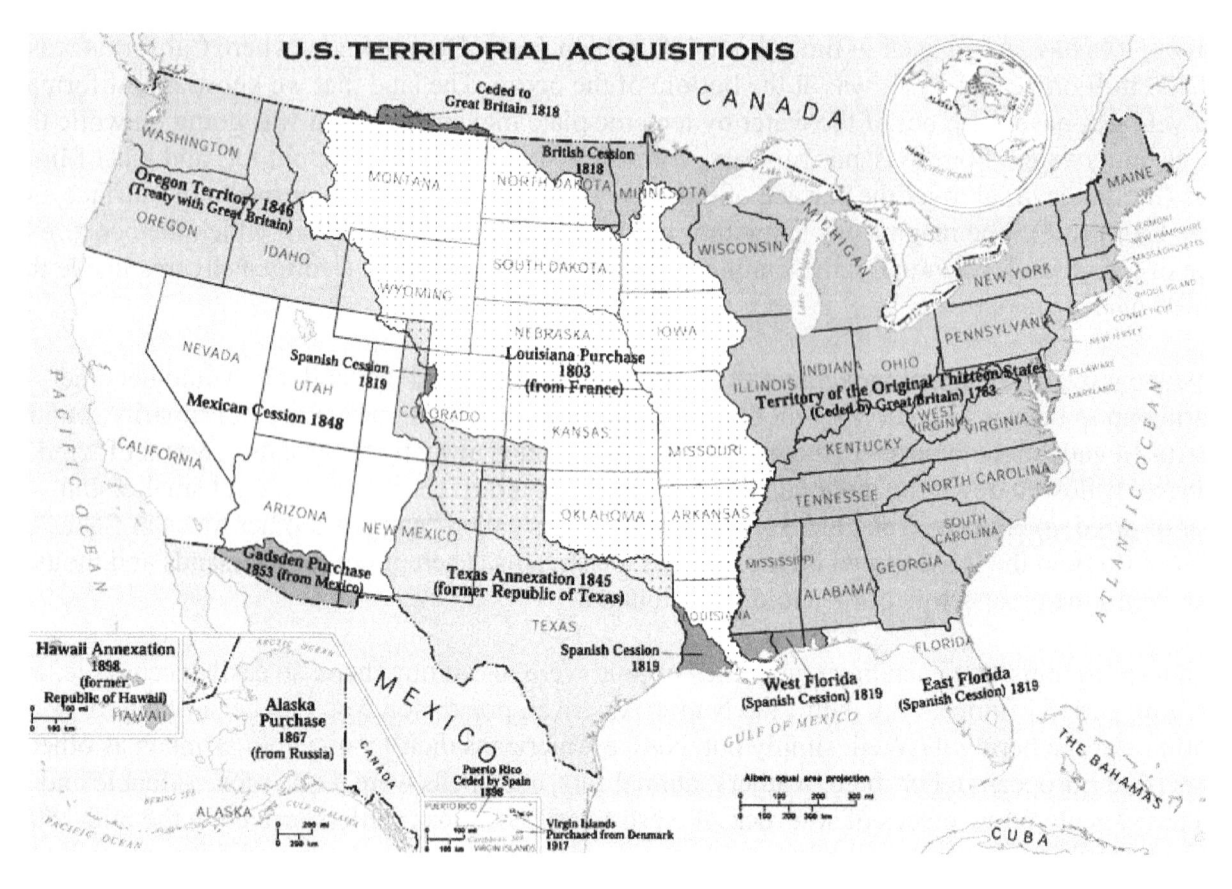

That's how the United States got ownership of California. At first, it was mainly military personnel who lived there, as it was not officially a state or even a territory yet. It was simply a piece of acquired land that had to be organized and explored a little bit at a time. There were some Europeans and Americans already living there when the treaty was signed, however. For some time, Mexican officials had been allowing small groups of pioneers (men who went to isolated areas to settle them) to explore California and to set up small farms and forts there. By 1848, about 1,000 settlers were living in California, mainly in the San Francisco bay area. One such man was John Sutter.

John Sutter, original born Johann August Sutter in Germany, came to California in 1839. In August of that year, he began to build a fort that he named after himself. It was near the Sacramento River in Northern California, about 90 miles away from San Francisco. After establishing friendly relations with the local tribes of Native Americans (the Maidu and the Miwok tribes) Sutter decided to focus on farming, raising livestock, and on making a profit from the abundant natural resources to be found. In 1848, he formed a partnership with James W. Marshall to build a sawmill. This mill would process local trees into usable wood for later sale (and a nice profit). The sawmill, built near the modern day town of Coloma, would be powered by the American River that it was built beside.

Because of his experience, James Marshall was in charge of the actual mill construction while Sutter stayed in his fort and focused on his business there.

SUTTER'S MILL AT COLOMA
A reproduction of photograph in possession of Charles B. Turrill, of San Francisco, from original daguerreotype taken on the spot by R. H. Vance in 1850. James W. Marshall in the foreground.

While looking over the progress of the mill on the morning of January 24, 1848, Marshall noticed some shiny yellow flakes trapped in the lower part of the mill where the river water was flowing through. He showed them to Sutter, and they did some basic tests on the metal to see what it was. The test confirmed it: they had found gold.

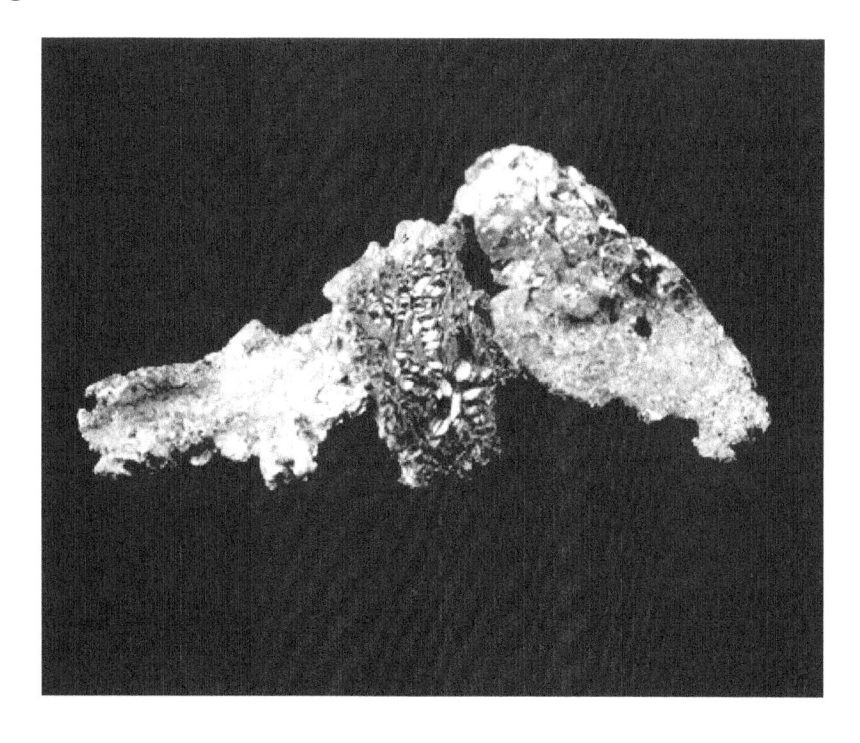

At first, no one could believe that gold was just sitting there, waiting for someone to go and pick it up. Most of the people who heard about the story (even though Sutter and Marshall tried to keep it a secret) thought it was just a hoax or a rumor. Sutter started trying to buy up the land around the mill so that he could legally claim the gold, and Marshall decided to keep working on the sawmill itself. However, news of the gold discovery could not be contained for long. Marshall's men began looking for gold during their breaks. Another man from nearby San Francisco (which was called "Yerba Buena" in those days) walked up and down the streets, telling the 1,000 or so inhabitants that gold had been found in the American River. This man, Samuel Brannan, wasn't as interested in finding gold himself as he was in selling supplies to interested miners. He became one of the richest men during the Gold Rush, most of his money coming from being a good salesman with an eye for opportunity.

As ships came into the San Francisco port, they travelled back to the east coast, and the passengers told the people there all about the massive amounts of gold in California. In the meantime, nearby residents from Oregon and Mexico began heading to California to get some gold for themselves. By August, New York newspapers were reporting Marshall's gold discovery. In December, President James Polk spoke about and confirmed the discovery to Congress during his State of the union address. Admitting that even he himself thought that the first reports were a hoax, he then said:

> "The explorations already made warrant the belief that the supply is very large and that gold is found at various places in an extensive district of country."[7]

This official confirmation from the President of the United States was enough to make thousands upon thousands of people leave everything behind and make the trip to California. The Gold Rush had begun.

Chapter 2: Why did the Gold Rush happen?

As you can imagine, a find of this much gold would make everyone living nearby get very excited. Sutter himself had to have been very happy to think about the gold that was on his land. However, the question that we want is answered is this: why did people go so crazy about the discovery of gold? Nowadays, if you hear about someone finding oil, gold, or diamonds, do you pack up everything and run to try to find some for yourself? Of course not! Then what made everyone back then leave their entire lives behind to go and look for gold? There were two main reasons why the Gold Rush happened like it did: the issue of **land ownership in California** and the **attitude of Americans at the time**. Let's look closer at these two factors.

Land ownership in California. As you may recall from the previous section, California in 1848 was not yet a state or even an organized U.S. territory. It was simply a piece of land acquired by the government that had yet to be explored and divided. There was no government, no courts, no police, and no land owners. When gold was discovered, there was no one to decide who could work on what piece on land. In other words: it was a free-for-all. The first person who arrived could "stake his claim" (fix his own land boundaries) anywhere he wanted. If he didn't see results, he would move on to another area and do the same.

---

[7] James Polk gold quote: http://www.findingdulcinea.com/news/on-this-day/On-This-Day--President-Polk-Sparks-the-California-Gold-Rush.html

This idea, the notion of arriving and setting up camp anywhere you wanted with gold just waiting to be found, captured the imagination of people across the world. It was just too good to pass up. However, land ownership issues weren't the only factors that contributed to the Gold Rush. There were others.

Attitude of Americans at the time. When the first settlers came to America and established the Jamestown colony back in 1607, they quickly learned that the best way to make money in the New World wasn't any sort of get-rich-quick scheme; the best way was spending long years doing hard work and showing determination. For centuries, that was the American dream: buy your land, build your house, raise your family, and build your fortune over a lifetime.

The Gold Rush changed all of that. The new American dream became getting rich overnight by striking it rich in California. This attitude helped to fuel the fire that became the Gold Rush. However, there was something else involved, something that involved President James Polk himself: a philosophy called "Manifest Destiny". Have you ever heard of that philosophy before?

As you know, American colonists first settled on the East coast of the United States. As time went by, they settled northwards and southwards, and then began to push westward. But, there were a few obstacles to their westward advancement: a lot of the land west of the Mississippi River already had owners: nations like France, Spain, Mexico, and Britain, not to mention the hundreds of thousands of Native Americans who had lived there for generations, who would defend their land ownership. However, in the American psyche (way of thinking) there was something very special about the land of North America: it was destined to belong to the United States, coast to coast, sea to shining sea. No one else could ever be its owner.

Although the idea had been around for a while, one journalist named John L. O'Sullivan really explained this philosophy clearly in an article he wrote talking about ownership of Oregon on December 27, 1845, a few years before the Gold Rush started. He said:

> "And that claim is by the right of our manifest destiny to overspread and to possess the whole of the continent which Providence has given us for the development of the great experiment of liberty and federated self-government entrusted to us."[8]

This philosophy, which came to be called "Manifest Destiny" after the phrase coined by O'Sullivan, came to influence some of the important decisions made by President James Polk himself. During his inaugural address in 1845, he said:

> "...It is confidently believed that our system may be safely extended to the utmost bounds of our territorial limits and that as it shall be extended the bonds of our Union, so far from being weakened, will become stronger..."[9]

This attitude of Manifest Destiny shaped his presidency. How so? For example, as we saw earlier, President Polk was not afraid of going to war with Mexico over the state of Texas. Why not? Because he felt that the United States was *destined* to own land all the way to the Pacific Ocean, including Texas. The Treaty of Guadalupe Hidalgo that ended the Mexican American War made Polk and other Americans very happy because it was giving them the land that they felt America was already entitled to

[8] John L. O'Sullivan quote source: http://en.wikipedia.org/wiki/Manifest_destiny#cite_note-3
[9] Source for James Polk's quote: http://www.learningfromlyrics.org/manifest.html

When gold was discovered in California, this little frontier outpost became the focus of worldwide attention. However, Americans themselves especially felt a special desire to go. After all, it was their *destiny* to get all the riches that the New World had to offer, including the gold of California.

As we have seen, several factors (not only the value of gold itself) contributed to making to the Gold Rush such a large phenomenon. What actually happened during the Gold Rush? Let's find out.

Chapter 3: What happened during the Gold Rush?

During the Gold Rush, the population of California exploded. It went from about 1,000 settlers to over 300,000 within a few short years, with some 90,000 prospectors coming west in 1849 alone. Cities were built almost overnight, and sometimes they were abandoned just as quickly. Local governments were quickly organized and began to bring some law and order to the chaotic lifestyle of the miners and prospectors. Let's have a closer look at some different aspects of life during the Gold Rush. We will look at the following areas:

- **The people who came to find gold**
- **The methods used to find gold**
- **Some problems faced by prospectors**
- **Surprising facts about the Gold Rush**

Are you ready to learn more about what happened during the Gold Rush? Then let's continue.

The people who came to find gold. James Marshall found gold at Sutter's Mill in January of 1848. Within a short time, settlers living in San Francisco and as far away as Oregon heard about the discovery and came running, picks and hammers in hand, to claim their share. The ones who arrived first, in 1848, found ideal conditions for finding gold. The gold was easy to locate, and required very little work to get to it. There were hardly any other prospectors around (meaning there wasn't a lot of competition) and most of the gold hadn't been found yet.

For the prospectors who came in 1849 (called the forty-niners) things weren't quite as easy. By the time they arrived, most of the good pieces of land had already been claimed. The gold that was just sitting in the gravel along the rivers and streams had already been found, and there were lots more people now fighting to find their share. In fact, the large amount of people moving to California had raised the prices of everything in the cities. San Francisco had grown so much that they actually ran out of space to build any more new houses. A solution that they came up with was to create a landfill of garbage and rocks and to dump it into the bay. This was done, and it provided more surface area for houses and shops.

Other towns sprung up almost overnight. These towns, called "boom towns" would form around an area that was thought to have a lot of gold. Prospectors would come running and merchants would come running after them. Houses and shops would be built, and the town would bustle for a few years or maybe a little more. However, after the gold supply had run out, the prospectors would move on, and the merchants would go with them. The town would suddenly become very quiet. The large empty buildings and the lonely, deserted streets became a familiar sight during the Gold Rush, and these places came to be called "ghost towns".

The people who came to look for gold also had to face all kinds of dangers. These dangers began on the actual trip out to California. In 1849 there was no railroad service to California (and of course no airplanes) so the only way to get to the gold was either by land (with horse and wagon) or by sea. In fact, it was divided about fifty-fifty: about half came by sea and the other half by land. To come by sea meant getting on a ship on the east coast and making the dangerous trip down around the southern tip of South America. For those who weren't brave enough to try that route, they could always sail to the Isthmus of Panama, cross the overland route on donkeys (or walking) and wait for a ship headed north to the port of San Francisco.

The overland route meant crossing the Rocky Mountains and then the Sierra Nevada mountain range, which was not an easy feat even for experienced travelers. Some who had recently tried to cross the Sierra Nevada got stuck in deep snow for the entire winter of 1846 in the Donner Pass. With very little food and no hope of rescue, this party became notorious among settlers because some of them actually resorted to eating fellow dead travelers. Stories like this made some people think twice about travelling over land. No everybody was deterred, and thousands kept on going west because they wanted that California gold.

Once arriving in California, there were different types of dangers to worry about. There was disease, cave-ins at gold mines, violence in the streets, and so on. In fact, one out of every twelve people that went west during the Gold Rush died within a short time. It was not an easy way of life, but for many it was worth it to get as much gold as they could.

The methods used to find gold. At first, there wasn't a lot of technology required to find gold in California; it had more to do with being in the right place at the right time and with being willing to do lots of hard work. Let's look at some of the methods used during the Gold Rush to collect that gold.

- Placer mining. This was the first and most popular type of mining during the Gold Rush. "Placer" is from a Spanish word that refers to the "shoal", or shallow banks, of a river. It was in these gravel-covered shoals that many of the loose gold nuggets and leaves were to be found. There were several ways that a miner could look for gold in these areas working by himself: he could use a pan with ridges to swish the gravel around, letting the heavy gold settle at the bottom, or he could use a "rocker" to sift through larger quantities of gravel.

- Hydraulic mining. After all of the gold near the rivers and creeks had been found, prospectors had to start looking harder for California's gold. First used in 1853, this method proved to be one of the most productive; and the most destructive. By the time that it was banned in 1884, an estimated 11 million ounces of gold were discovered and sold. How did hydraulic mining work?

    The goal of hydraulic mining was to loosen the gold that might be buried in hillsides. Large pumps were brought in to blast hillsides with strong streams of water. The dirt and rocks from the hill fell to the ground and were carried away to a sluice (a miniature aqueduct) where the heavy gold would fall to the bottom. This method was banned in 1884 because of the large quantities of dirt and ore that were washing into the San Francisco Bay.

- Hard rock mining. This is the method that we saw described in the introduction, where men would use dynamite to blast deep into the earth, looking for strains of gold hidden in hard rock (which was usually quartz in California). This was also a dangerous method for the miners. The tunnels could collapse at any moment, dangerous gases could suffocate them, or the water pumps could stop working and they could all drown in the groundwater. Despite the danger, some 60% of the gold extracted during the Gold Rush was from hard rock mining techniques.

Some of the problems faced by prospectors. As if it weren't hard enough to travel thousands of miles and to work ten hour days one mile underground, prospectors had other problems to worry about. For example, do you remember who was living in California before the thousands upon thousands of gold seekers arrived? Well, there were the "Californios", the former Mexican citizens now living in the United States territory known as California. But there were also thousands and thousands of Native Americans, organized into various tribes. In 1845, there were about 150,000 Native Americans (although there would only be 30,000 by 1870). For generations, these tribes had lived off of the land and had fished in the waters. Now, this was the same land and the same water that were being taken away from them or that was being polluted by prospectors. How do you think the Native Americans felt?

As you can imagine, the native people (both Native Americans and Californios) did not appreciate being pushed around and kicked off of their lands. Many Native Americans, away from the only lands and food sources that they had ever known, died of starvation. Others resisted and fought back against the prospectors, which brought even greater violence. For example, one settler named Colonel John Anderson was killed in the spring of 1852 in Northern California by a local Wintu Native American group. The group stole his livestock (most likely to feed themselves after having lost their hunting grounds) and ran away. Soon after the murder, 70 men led by Sherriff William H. Dixon hunted down the local Wintu tribe and killed all but three (small children) of the 150 member tribe. As they got closer, however, they saw that the murderers of the Colonel were not among the dead. They had killed the wrong people.

Fights like these (between settlers and Native Americans) were common, and it was the Native Americans who usually ended up losing. That being said, it was also common for the prospectors of different races and nationalities to fight among themselves. Coming from so many different nations, including China and Australia, non-American gold seekers were taxed heavily and taken advantage of.

Surprising facts about the Gold Rush. While newspaper reports often talked about how much gold was found during the Gold Rush, and how many prospectors struck it big, gold seekers weren't the ones who made the most money during those years- it was the merchants who really filled their pockets. As an example, do you remember the San Francisco business named Samuel Brannan who publicized Sutter and Marshall's discovery of gold? Seeing an opportunity (and predicting the coming Gold Fever) Samuel went out and bought up all of the mining equipment in the whole city. Then, he happily sold it to interested prospectors- for a much higher price than he paid for it. He became San Francisco's first millionaire.

Like Samuel Brannan, many other merchants (not only in San Francisco but also in the many other boomtowns) got rich by taking care of the needs of gold seekers. Some built hotels and lodging houses while others focused on sewing, cleaning laundry, providing entertainment, or even on making and selling clothes. For example, cotton blue jeans had become very popular during the Gold Rush because they were durable and easy to take care of. Beginning in 1873, Levi Strauss made his fortune selling high-quality work pants to forty-niners in San Francisco.

Another surprising fact has to do with the number of women and children that participated in the Gold Rush. Although we normally think of men working hard to get gold, there were also entire families that spent their days placer mining alongside streams and rivers. Later on, with the population boom, women came west to find adventure or to work. Because prospectors valued a woman's touch on their clothes, such women would sometimes set up a business and charge high prices to do a quality job of washing and ironing a man's clothes. Some of these women were widows, others had their husbands, but they all loved the life that came from living in the Wild West.

Chapter 4: What was it like to be a kid during the Gold Rush?

As we have seen so far, living during the Gold Rush meant a lot of hard work and a lot of danger. Can you imagine seeing so much danger and death around you? Well, have you ever known someone that died? Back then, remember that one out of every twelve people who went to California during the Gold Rush died. Imagine that today: out of every twelve people that you know, one dies suddenly. It would have been terrible to see so many people getting into accidents and getting sick.

More than just worrying about other people, however, you would also have had to worry a lot about yourself. For example, what would you have done if you found a lot of gold? Would you have been able to trust anybody to help you work the area, or would you have been too afraid to tell anyone about it? What would you have done with the gold once you had dug it up out of the ground? After all, there were lots of thieves back then. Can you understand how the Gold Rush made some people less trusting of others?

Another concern was establishing good relationships with Native Americans. It may sound easy, but there was a big problem for prospectors who were looking for gold: Native Americans were living on much of the land that had lots of gold on it. What would have been the best way to handle the situation? A lot of prospectors ended up using force to remove the Native American tribes from their lands, while others used outright violence. Do you think that it was right of them to do that? What would you have done? While it may be easy to think that we would have just made friends with the local Native American tribes, what if they didn't want to leave? At what point does a desire to be rich become more important than the way that we treat other people? Because of their dream of getting rich quickly, a lot of prospectors did some pretty terrible things to other people.

Being so far away from civilization, it was not uncommon to see people get really sick from strange diseases. When you are sick, do you go to the doctor? Of course you do, we all do! But imagine living far away from the nearest city. If you get sick, there may not be anyone to help you. What if you came across a bear or a mountain lion in the woods? What would you do? These were all very real dangers for the people looking for gold in California.

Kids living back then were also used to working hard. Think about the deep gold mine that we learned about in the introduction: Empire Gold Mine near Grass Valley, California. That is a real mine, and you can still visit it today and see what it was like to work there. Did you know that there were donkeys that spent their entire lives down inside that mine, working long hours and carrying heavy carts full of rocks and gold? Well, there were some men who spent their lives like those donkeys. They spent long days underground and got tired, dirty, and sweaty trying to get rich. Even if they found lots of gold, it was the owners of the mine who would usually keep most of it; for the workers themselves, it was just another day on the job. The American Dream of striking it rich disappeared after the first few years of the Gold Rush; after that, looking for gold was just another type of work, like a being in a factory.

Would you have liked to be alive back then? Although there was a chance that you might get rich overnight, most people only made enough money to just get by. A lot more went home even poorer than when they started. Their dreams of striking it rich in California never came true.

Chapter 5: How did the Gold Rush end?

Simply put, the Gold Rush ended when the gold ran out.

Throughout the years that it lasted, the prospectors had tried different methods as the gold got harder and harder to find. They started with placer mining in order to get the gold that was easy to find (buried in the gravel of river banks). Then, they began using hydraulic mining to blast away entire hillsides to get to the gold buried beneath. After that, others would go downstream to dredge through the ore and rocks that had been removed by past operations, just in case any gold had slipped through. Finally, prospectors moved on to hard rock mining. This method continued to be used to find gold in California for almost one hundred years (until the 1950s) when most of the mines were shut down because they were no longer profitable.

Because of the vast amounts of money coming from California, it was admitted as into the Union in 1850, as a free state. Billions of dollars were shipped out (in the form of gold) to the east coast, much of it ending up in the hands of the government.

Many of the people who had migrated to California to look for gold ended up staying and finding other ways of making money. Some opened schools, became politicians, started businesses, and built permanent homes. Instead of being a bunch of rowdy prospectors looking for fun and a quick dollar, Californians became like citizens of any other state: families, tradesmen, farmers, and so on.

The large migration of people to California had also done a lot to open up transportation and communication with the area. The Pony Express (mounted riders who would carry correspondence and packages all the way from Missouri to San Francisco) operated from 1860 to 1861, after which telegraph wires were installed. Soon after that, railroad tracks would follow (starting in 1863), and many of the same workers that had worked hard looking for gold would work hard blasting tunnels in the Sierra Nevada and Rocky Mountains and laying miles upon miles of train tracks.

For example, many of the Chinese workers that had come to California looking for gold were hired to help build the transcontinental railroad. They worked long hours both in the hot sun and during the freezing winter. Some lost their lives during huge dynamite explosions in the tunnels while others were buried in avalanches in the two mountain ranges. Their labor made the railroad a success, even finishing it about seven years ahead of schedule. If it weren't for the Gold Rush, these Chinese workers would never have come to California.

The Gold Rush had ended, but its effects would last for a very long time.

Chapter 6: What happened after the Gold Rush?

Any time you deal with large amounts of people and money, you can be sure that important things will happen as a result. Some of the effects of the Gold Rush were felt right away, others a little later, and some are still seen today. Let's see what happened after the Gold Rush, and how it changed a lot of things about the United States.

One of the first effects was a very negative one: many Native Americans died. This happened in a variety of ways: disease, relocation, outright violence.

Disease: When settlers came to California searching for gold, they found about 150,000 Native Americans living and hunting and gathering and raising their families, just as they had been doing for countless generations. However, the first meetings between settlers and Native Americans ended up with many of the Native Americans dying of strange new diseases. How did that happen? As you may know, our bodies protect us against diseases by being exposed to just a little bit of it, especially in the cases of viruses. However, if a person is exposed to large quantities of a new virus, the body often cannot fight off the disease and the person ends up dying very quickly. This is what happened to large numbers of Native Americans in California. With all of the new settlers arriving from so many countries with so many different types of viruses, the immune systems of the native population just could not handle all of the strange new diseases, and they died in large numbers.

Relocation: As we saw earlier, Native Americans were already living on lands that were rich with the very gold that prospectors wanted. When they arrived in beginning in 1848, some of these prospectors forced whole tribes to leave these lands, the only ones that they had ever known. The Native American tribes had to go to new places where they couldn't find food, couldn't raise crops, and had no place to care for their animals. Being forced from one place to another, many Native Americans actually ended up starving to death, with no one to help them. Can you believe that some people could have been so cruel like that?

Outright violence: As tensions between the two groups got stronger and stronger with each passing year, some Native Americans began to retaliate, or fight back, against the harsh and unfair treatment that they were receiving. As you can imagine, this only made those hateful prospectors angrier and crueler. We already saw what happened at the Bridge Gulch Massacre. However, that was not the only violence against Native Americans that happened during the Gold Rush. Another massacre that took place in 1850 was called the Bloody Island Massacre. This happened when a group of enslaved Pomo people revolted and murdered their cruel masters. In retaliation, almost 25% of the group (about 100) was killed by a regiment of the United States cavalry. Sadly, there were other massacres like these.

The terrible treatment of Native Americans was one of the terrible effects of the Gold Rush. Although there had been around 150,000 Native Americans in California in 1845, before gold was discovered, there were only 30,000 by 1870, only twenty five years later.

Another long term effect was unfortunately also a negative one. Do you remember some of the methods that were used by prospectors trying to find gold? After they had found a lot of gold using placer mining, they began to use hydraulic mining methods. This is when they would blast entire hillsides with powerful streams of water to knock the rocks (and the gold inside it) loose. As the dirt, rocks, and gold fell into the streams of water below, the heavy wood would be caught in the sluices set up by the prospectors, and the sand and gravel would be washed away into the rivers.

As all of this sediment moved down the rivers, much of it ended up either in the Sacramento Valley or in the San Francisco Bay area. The changes in the river paths and the raised level of the ground had a sort of domino effect that led to major flooding each spring, which absolutely devastated towns in the Sacramento Valley. What's more, the hillsides themselves lost valuable topsoil and, as a result, nothing could grow there anymore. Sadly, these effects have lasted to this day. In the picture below, you can see a recent picture taken in Northern California of a former hydraulic mining site.

Also, some of the methods of extracting gold used dangerous elements to make it easier to separate from the surrounding water and dirt. For example, one website explains how mercury, a dangerous element in large quantities, was used in gold mining:

> "To enhance gold recovery from hydraulic mining, hundreds of pounds of liquid mercury (several 76-lb flasks) were added to riffles and troughs in a typical sluice. The high density of mercury allowed gold and gold-mercury amalgam to sink while sand and gravel passed over the mercury and through the sluice. Large volumes of turbulent water flowing through the sluice caused many of the finer gold and mercury particles to wash through and out of the sluice before they could settle in the mercury-laden riffles. A modification known as an undercurrent (fig. 5) reduced this loss. The finer grained particles were diverted to the undercurrent, where gold was amalgamated on mercury-lined copper plates. Most of the mercury remained on the copper plates; however, some was lost to the flowing slurry and was transported to downstream environments."[10]

---
[10] Mercury mining source: http://pubs.usgs.gov/fs/2005/3014/

This mercury later went on to contaminate streams and even the ocean, where it is still present today. For this reason, we have to be careful how much fish we eat and even what kinds, because of the mercury used during the Gold Rush.

Another effect of the Gold Rush was the large amount of money received by the Federal Government. At the time, money was printed based on the amount of gold in government safes. As they received more gold, more money was printed, and spending power of the average American increased. Some of this money from the Gold rush later went on to supply weapons, uniforms, and equipment to the Union Army during the Civil War that broke out fifteen years later. How important were these extra funds? The superior funding of the Northern Army was one of the deciding factors of the Civil War, something which completely changed U.S. history and led to the abolishment of slavery. If it had not been for the Gold Rush and all of the money that it brought to the U.S. government, who knows if the Civil War would have ended differently?

Finally, another long term effect of the Gold Rush was the diversity that we see in California today. This is perhaps one of the best results, bringing together so many different types on people together in one place. It has contributed to making California a popular place to go for art, entertainment, agriculture, and culinary artistry (which means good food for us).

These effects, whether short term or long term, were all directly related to the discovery of gold in 1848 and of the Gold Rush that followed.

Conclusion

When James Marshall found a few flakes of gold while working on Sutter's Mill that January morning, do think that he had any idea what would be the consequences? Could he have possibly imagined that his discovery would indirectly lead to a population boom in California, to the deaths of thousands of Native Americans, to the invention of new technologies, to the construction of the Transcontinental Railroad, or that it would even affect the outcome of a future Civil War? Is there any way that he could have known that thousands and thousands of people would have their lives turned upside down- sometimes for good, sometimes for bad- by this one little discovery? Oddly enough, James Marshall never really benefitted from his discovery, and even died a poor man some years later.

The Gold Rush brought out the best and worst in the people who participated. It brought out great business skills in men like Samuel Brannan; but it also brought out the ruthless cruelty in those who committed massacres against both Native American landowners and against Chinese miners. The desire to make money even led to unfortunate environmental consequences which we are still suffering today.

When you look at the overall picture, what do you think: was the Gold Rush a good thing or a bad thing for the United States and for the world? If you had been alive back then, would you have been one of the people running to find gold of your own or would you have been content to let others go and just to hear about their adventures?

Important things often start with little events. And as was the case with the Gold Rush, it was the first people who acted who benefitted the most. What about you? Will you be quick to take advantage of an opportunity when you see it? Will you try to see the big picture and look at the possible consequences of your actions? Will you think about other people before making big decisions? These are all valuable lessons to be learned from the Gold Rush, the race that changed the United States.